BEYOND HATE

LIVING With Our DIFFERENCES

Eamonn Deane and Carol Rittner

Editors

© YES! Publications

Derry

Commissioned by the Centre for Creative Communications, Derry, with
support from Mutual of America and the International Fund for Ireland.

First edition, 1994
Published in Northern Ireland by
Yes! Publications
10 - 12 Bishop Street
Derry
Northern Ireland
BT48 6PW

ISBN 1 873832 04 4

Printed by Coleraine Printing Company
Tel: 54873 / 58412

♲ Printed on recycled paper
Cover Design by Michael McCarron/Joe Campbell

To the memory
of all those who have died
in 'The Troubles'
during the last twenty-five years

One of our problems as human beings is that we have very good memories. People carry their memories for many years, sometimes across generations. Whenever there is a situation where people have something traumatic to remember, at the first opportunity they use those memories to give credence to atrocities and hate. The problem we face is how to start a new chapter? How can we say, "Let bygones be bygones?" We need to open a new chapter, even as all the old memories are lurking in the shadows, just waiting to express themselves.

When a person tries to overcome a trauma, there is no way for that person to close the old chapter and open a new one without some type of reckoning with what has gone before. Repentance, or some type of accounting, has to precede the ability to close one chapter and start another. Individuals need to do this, but so, too, do groups and nations. It is not enough to find a political accommodation. The language of accommodation also is needed, language that gives individuals, groups, and nations the possibility of closing one chapter and starting a new one, unshackled from the trauma of the past

Shlomo Breznitz
Israel

CONTENTS

• Books by Eamonn Deane •

LOST HORIZONS, NEW HORIZONS:
Community Development in Northern Ireland
(ed.) 1989.

• Books by Carol Rittner •

THE COURAGE TO CARE
(ed. with Sondra Myers), 1986.

ELIE WIESEL:
Between Memory and Hope
(ed.), 1990.

MEMORY OFFENDED:
The Auschwitz Convent Controversy
(ed. with John K. Roth), 1991.

DIFFERENT VOICES:
Women and the Holocaust
(ed. with John Roth),
1993.

BEYOND THE DIARY:
Anne Frank in the World
(ed.), 1993.

Acknowledgements

During the September 1992 *Beyond Hate: Living With Our Deepest Differences* conference, the American improvisational pianist, John Bayless, gave a concert to an enthusiastic audience of conference participants and guests. His repertoire ranged from Beethoven to Gershwin, from *We Shall Overcome* to *Danny Boy*. Bayless captivated his audience. His ability to go 'beyond' familiar music, to create 'new' music from 'different' musical scores was an artistic metaphor challenging us to find concrete ways to move 'beyond hate' and learn how to 'live with our deepest differences'.

Uniquely gifted, John Bayless touched our humanity. People were in harmony, at least momentarily. When the concert ended, an appreciative audience gratefully acknowledged him and his contribution. We, too, want to thank John Bayless for his part in the *Beyond Hate* conference, and we also want to acknowledge and thank all those who have participated in and contributed to the entire project and to the publication of this volume.

Elie Wiesel, the 1986 Nobel Peace Laureate, began *The Anatomy of Hate* project in 1987, just after receiving the Nobel prize. His example and commitment to exploring 'the anatomy of hate' inspired the 'beyond hate' project in Derry. In an effort to provide some continuity, we have incorporated into the present book short excerpts from presentations given at earlier conferences by Shlomo Breznitz (Boston, 1989), Gro Harlem Bruntland (Oslo, 1990), Leo Eitinger (Boston, 1989), Claire Gaudiani (Haifa, 1990), Nelson Mandela (Oslo, 1990), John K. Roth (Haifa, 1990), Wole Soyinka (Paris, 1988), Romila Thapar (Oslo, 1990), and Professor Wiesel (Oslo, 1990). All other contributions were made either in person or through the medium of video during the 1992-93 *Beyond Hate* programme.

William J. Flynn, Chairman of the Board, Mutual of America, New York, NY, USA, from the beginning worked closely with Elie Wiesel to make possible *The Anatomy of Hate* project. Mr. Flynn's support, and that of Mutual of America, also made possible the 1992 *Beyond Hate* project in Derry, Northern Ireland. Without his enthusiastic encouragement, sound advice, and participation, neither the Derry project nor this book, *Beyond Hate: Living With Our Differences* would have been made possible.

We also give special thanks to the International Fund for Ireland for their generous support for this publication. We thank SIPTU (Service Industrial Professional Technical Union), the Northern Ireland Community Relations Council, and the Central Community Relations Unit for their support of the *Beyond Hate* project. Derry City Council, Fruit of the Loom, and the Sisters of Mercy (Derry Diocese) also provided needed support.

Every project requires teamwork, and we could not have carried it out or completed this book without the assistance of many people, among whom we count Mary Canavan and her staff at the Centre for Creative Communications, Mairead Browne, Roma Casey, John Geary, Ciaran Nelis and Andrea Pistor. Rosa Gallagher and her staff at the Inner City Trust typing pool assisted us, as did Liam Browne, Catherine Browne and Martin Kiffer. Likewise, we want to thank Martina Millar, Hugh Gallagher, Joe Campbell, and Peter Townsend at Holywell Trust for their assistance. We thank Don Mullan for arranging Desmond Tutu's video address to the conference and all of those people who gave their time, energy and generosity during the workshops, seminars, lectures and the conference itself. We thank Alan Colhoun, Danny McGinley and the staff of young photographers from Derry Youth and Community Workshop. We also thank James Canavan, and the local press: *Derry Journal, Londonderry Sentinel, Belfast Telegraph*. We thank the staff of Bookworm for their ever-willing support and assistance. Bridget O'Toole gave invaluable advice and support during the final proof reading. To all those who helped make this volume possible, especially the participants in the September 1992 *Beyond Hate* conference, we are grateful.

Eamonn Deane and Carol Rittner, R.S.M. are responsible for editing the words of those who participated in the conference. We hope we have been faithful both to the letter and to the spirit of what was said. If we have inadvertently distorted someone's words, we profoundly apologise. If we have succeeded in faithfully editing the conference discussion and presentation, we are grateful. If this book is well received, it will be because of the dedication and hard work of Simone Horner and Michael McCarron who ever so carefully typed and re-typed the text into the computer, who skillfully and graciously helped to design and produce the book. They assured the publication of *Beyond Hate: Living With Our Differences*. Our gratitude is without measure.

Finally, we want to thank the new government of South Africa for permission to reproduce as the book's Afterword a portion of President Nelson Mandela's inaugural speech. Just as John Bayless artistically touched the common humanity of all of us — women and men, Protestant and Catholic, Black and White, Asian and European, American and African, Arab and Jew, British and Irish — so Nelson Mandela, by his life and his words, has inspired human beings the world over to 'try again' to create a more humane world that will embrace 'differences' so that there will be "justice for all... peace for all... work, bread, water and salt for all."

Preface

Eamonn Deane
Northern Ireland

Carol Rittner
USA

It began with a telephone call in September 1990 to the office of The Elie Wiesel Foundation for Humanity in New York City. Dr. Carol Rittner, R.S.M., then the Foundation's Director, took the call. Some people in Derry wanted to organise a conference about 'hate', similar to the one that they read about in the newspapers that had been held in Oslo, Norway a few weeks previously. Could Dr. Rittner help? Would she come to Northern Ireland and talk to Paddy Doherty, Kevin McCaul, Eamonn Deane, John Shiels, Paddy Walley, and Terry Doherty?

Carol Rittner, who was about to leave The Wiesel Foundation to finish several books, agreed to come to the North of Ireland at the end of November 1990. She was so unfamiliar with the island's history that when she tried to get a flight into 'Derry', she was told by the travel agent who was trying to book her flight that there was no city with the name 'Derry' in Northern Ireland. There was, however, a city named 'Londonderry'. Could it be the place she wanted to go?

Mention Paris, London, Rome, Tokyo, New York, or Jerusalem and people know where they are; airplanes know how to fly there. Mention a city with two names — like the one some call 'Derry', others 'Londonderry' — emblematic of how two peoples with shared roots, Catholics and Protestants, have dealt with their history — and you reveal your 'politics'. It is a city with two unique, inalienable, and intertwined strengths: its history and its location. It has been bedeviled and blessed by both. It is a city away to the northwest of the island of Ireland, a place on the periphery of Europe. It is a city that has played an important role in Europe's history throughout the centuries. And it is also a City that is one of the flashpoints of the political activism marking the latter half of twentieth century European history. Each phase of its history has left its mark on the city and on the consciousness of its people. The result is a cultural heritage rich in diversity, filled with potential for engendering conflict, and relevant to contemporary world affairs.

Nowhere are people more aware of their heritage, whether recent or distant; nowhere are they more conscious of their ancestors' triumphs and sufferings. There, people experience ancient antagonism; there, they also are struggling to find ways to accommodate each other's differences. To those who view 'Londonderry' as a microcosm of Northern Ireland, there is a sense that the current 'troubles' began in 'Derry', a sense that 'Derry' also might point the way to resolution, which was precisely why the Centre for Creative Communications wanted to organise a conference on the theme, *Beyond Hate: Living With Our Deepest Differences.*

Carol Rittner arrived in Northern Ireland on a cold, dreary Autumn day at the end of November 1990.
In September 1992, the international conference, *Beyond Hate: Living With Our Deepest Differences* was held in the Derry City Guildhall, with participants from twenty-five countries from around the world. The conference was the central part of a process which continues to the present through lectures, discussions, seminars, publications, and cultural exchanges.

This edited volume is our attempt to capture the richness and variety of the process, the letter and the spirit of the presentations and discussions, and to present it to you, the reader, in a form which allows you to use it in different ways. You may decide to use it sequentially, to follow the themes we have tried to weave together as unobtrusively as possible, or you may choose to dip into different readings, using them as refreshing meditations which stand alone. Although we have taken minor liberties with the material, we have tried to be careful, to be faithful to the substance of the various contributions while making editorial amendments for the sake of clarity. We take full responsibility for these changes and adaptations.

It is difficult to measure the impact that the *Beyond Hate* process and project have had, or will have, on its wide variety of participants. We do know that there have been many useful outcomes already, some more tangible than others. We think it has been good for the city to host the conference, for it drew attention to the ability of the people in a city perceived to be an 'outpost' far from the 'action', 'on the edge' of Europe to creatively organise this project. It has helped people in this beautiful city on the River Foyle to realise that they, too, live in a place which generates creative possibilities in the midst of seemingly intractable problems.

All over the world there seems to be savagery, fragmentation, ethnic and tribal conflict, exemplified by the chaos tearing apart former Yugoslavia, Rwanda, the Indian sub-continent, and the former Soviet Union. And we are still plagued with the animosity of twenty-five years of 'the troubles' in Northern Ireland. As we look around the world, things seem to be more chaotic, rather than less.

During the *Beyond Hate* conference, Shlomo Breznitz said that one of the problems human beings have is that we have very good memories. We carry them for many years, sometimes across generations. Where there is a crisis, these memories surface and give credence to atrocities and hates. The question he asked, "Is it possible to open a new door, to start a new chapter, at some point to say, 'let bygones be bygones'" remains valid — and a challenge to all of us.

In Northern Ireland, people tell different stories of the history of the island, of the origins of their confrontation, of the wars they have fought, and of the terrorism they have endured. Such stories are often used to justify present 'certainties' rather than moving the challenge of coexistence of getting 'beyond hate' and 'living with differences' forward. Indeed, they frequently impede it.

If the work of moving 'beyond hate', the work of coexistence in Northern Ireland, and around the world is to proceed, the spell of the past must be broken. There must be 'revisions', or at least challenges, to the many cherished and disabling self-images people in both communities guard so carefully. There must be a truce, for example, in the war over the past and for the dubious prize of being considered the most wronged victim. Feelings of rage that thrive on certainty must be laid to rest. Instead of fuelling resentment and revenge, memory must become the hope and pledge of the future.

We hope the contributions that follow will challenge and encourage you to continue working to make this fragile world of ours more just and humane. As the Jewish sage, Rabbi Tarfon reminds us, "You do not have to finish the work, but neither are you free to desist from engaging in it."

Foreword

LIVING WITH OUR DIFFERENCES

Seamus Deane

In his book, *A Theory of Justice*, the American political philosopher John Rawls wrote, "Justice is the first virtue of social institutions, just as truth is the first virtue of systems of thought." Rawls' book is one of the noblest achievements of the American imagination in the twentieth century. It is also a very western book. *A Theory of Justice* is a book whose premise is that there is something called the 'autonomous individual' and that the fate and destiny of the individual in society is to be understood in relation to a series of propositions — laws, rules, regulations, and principles — in light of which people can live in justice and harmony only in a principled and organized fashion, not by virtue of sentimental attachments.

I admire and agree with Rawls, but my admiration and respect is tempered by my experience of growing up in Derry, of being from the North of Ireland. My experience reveals something that neither Rawls nor the Western tradition either advocates or sufficiently takes into account: community, a reality characterised by the intermeshing and interconnecting mutual support which is soldered and held together as a result of people working in concert with each other for a purpose which transcends their individual selves. I also think most theories of community have a deeper root.

Many ideas of community are based, sometimes lethally, sometimes benignly, on the notion of common identity, an identity that is linguistic, racial, social, political, or gender-based. When people are in a position of weakness, one of the ways they try to overcome their position is by 'bonding', by finding ways to connect with each other, by embracing what we might call their 'identity', whether national or cultural. Such a common identity binds people together in a way that makes them more members of the community than merely autonomous individuals. In fact, what individuality they have derives primarily from their belonging to the community.

Such a notion of community is valuable. It is frequently embraced by people who have suffered various forms of oppression, who have been victimised by being stereotyped and caricatured, deprived of power and control over their own lives. Such stereotyping and caricaturing of people under its control is part of the standard technique of every imperial power that has ever been. Not only does it profoundly humiliate the victims, at the same time rendering them harmless and sometimes even 'lovable', but it also affects victimisers in that it short-circuits their ability to relate to those under their control as human beings like themselves.

There is a relationship among people that comes from their culture, but in order to realise that relationship people must come into possession of their culture. Oppression not only denies people possession of their culture, but it denies people possession of themselves. Oppression denies people the power to represent themselves, not just to others but to themselves as well.

There is a link between justice, understood as a feature of social and political institutions, and the power of self-representation. Justice is a concept; like all concepts, it has a history. Community is a concept, equally embedded in history. No community can speak of itself without speaking of and to its history. Historical understanding and memory are intrinsic to any functioning notion of community. But justice is a concept that operates at a much higher level of abstraction. It is a word that claims to embody a universalist appeal and recognition. When it does so, in its purest form, like the form advocated by John Rawls, it disengages itself from history.

Every community has to relocate an idea of justice within its own history. Otherwise, there is a felt rupture between the community's ability to represent itself in its own terms and its ability to realise itself in universal terms. This is an inescapable tension in society. But, in societies that have undergone oppression, especially at the hands of imperial powers that have managed to universalise their own history and their culture-bound systems of justice, the tension is especially grievous.

In many cases, this produces a situation in which the oppressed culture is granted a certain measure of self-representation — in art and literature, for instance— and no capacity for self-representation in other important areas — ethics or political institutions, for example. The consequence is that such cultures can be apparently over-developed in one area of representation and underdeveloped in another. This is a distortion that is not easily over-come. The importance of community politics is that it gives to such groups of people the opportunity to develop a vocabulary and a style of living that is coincident with their social experience. It gives voice to what is specific to them and in them rather than assuming that their politics should be founded on the very western and especially the Anglo-American concept of the unified, autonomous self— itself a historical construct that has almost lost contact with the enabling conditions that gave birth to it.

Ireland is a classic example of this dis-possession of self, of being denied a national and cultural identity. It's one of the many stories residing within the long history of Irish writers, at least over the last half millennium. Ireland has gone silent in Irish and eloquent in English. One sees in Irish writers repeatedly developing a relationship in their writing between people who suffer asphasia, who are inarticulate and lack the capacity to say who they are, and those charismatic heroes and heroines who are astonishingly gifted with eloquence and with the gift of tongues. Culturally, this is part of the story of Irish colonisation, as it is part of the story of every people and nation that have suffered colonisation

Can a community represent itself to itself so that it may represent itself to others, despite the static of political stereotypes? That is an important question for every people and nation who have struggled with colonialism and the issue of community. Ireland is probably closer to achieving this now than it has been for a long time, but it has taken most of the twentieth century and a variety of efforts, both political and cultural, to make this even faintly possible.

If that is where we are now, and I think it is, it is as a result of 'community politics'. It is a politics in which there has been an attempt — sometimes organised, sometimes random — to overcome an imposed cultural impoverishment and to recover a richness which we persuade ourselves we once possessed. It does not really matter if historically we possessed it or not. The desire to possess it is sufficient to recruit it into the future. But that kind of 'community politics' — which I think is central to the hope that the North of Ireland has about the future — does not marry easily with the kind of politics suggested by John Rawls and his idea of justice.

We know there are many states in the world — one does not have to travel very far from Derry to find them — that could not survive the incorporation into their systems of the principles of justice. They are of their nature incompatible with justice, and when injustice is legitimated and becomes part and parcel of everyday life, it breeds hatred which in turn breeds violence which then creates more injustice. After a while, we begin to speak only of 'differences' between various forms of injustice that characterise both the state and opposition to the state. When that happens, most people say, "a plague on both houses," for they have no desire to choose either. In my view, this is precisely where the problem and the challenge lie.

If our desire for a just system is built on the premise of the autonomous individual, an idea that caters to individual freedom in the American fashion, rather than on the premise of community, I do not think we will solve any of the political problems that face us on the island of Ireland. We have to recognise that the idea of the autonomous individual is a Western construct that has had a very long life. It is a very noble construct, but it is not necessarily applicable to every situation.

In the North of Ireland our situation is one in which the idea of community should take precedence over the idea of the autonomous individual. It is only when 'community politics' is helped to become civilised by efforts to move beyond hate that we will not take that short, dreadful step into the inferno of racial hatred, hostility, exclusion, and xenophobia. When we take the path of civilisation, when we retrieve our idea of culture and what constitutes us as a culture, we are able to wed our Irish cultural and political experience to the European, the Anglo-American and even the Asian experience. As the little known but admirable American poet Alan Duggan wrote, "Freedom is as mortal as tyranny." It is something everyone needs to remember.

Seamus Deane

Setting The Context

Nelson Mandela

When we speak about hatred in the world today, we should do so without fear or favour. We should have the courage and political will to be counted among those who stood for right in the face of overwhelming evil. In this respect, we cannot talk about human rights without addressing the sea of problems confronting our generation, especially hunger, homelessness, illiteracy, ignorance and disease…

We are living in times of great upheavals and great hope. The political landscape of our world is being transformed beyond recognition. The familiar landmarks are no longer there. We are pioneers of a new world. We should, and indeed must, steer humanity towards a new path, away from the pain and tribulations that have afflicted us for so long. This is a task that can no longer wait.

We seek to build a society wherein a person's colour will matter no more. A society in which all our people will be united in their diversity. In doing so, we are challenging the scourge of racism which is negating the humanity of the whole world. We are opposed to white domination as much as we are opposed to black domination. The solution to our problems does not lie in the enslavement of others; rather, it lies in our ability to free all, for in so doing, we shall be freeing ourselves…

We are painfully aware of the practice of religious intolerance in many parts of the world. We are deeply saddened by the revival of antisemitism, particularly in Europe. We should not and cannot fold our arms and allow the world to regress into yet another abyss of hatred. Religion should be the basis of cooperation and not a source of conflict. In this regard, South Africa is perhaps more fortunate than other countries. The overwhelming majority of our people who belong to varied religious denominations, continue as a united force to challenge apartheid. It is our intention and prayer to carry this cooperation with us, as we enter a new and democratic society. Never again should anyone be discriminated against, or persecuted simply because he or she belongs to a different religion.

Let us all march forward, confident that good is ultimately bound to triumph over evil. History has shown that the human race does not only have the capacity, but also the will to rise in defence of humanity. Let us do so now, and not relegate our collective responsibility to posterity.

Hatred is an ancient scourge which threatens to annihilate humanity. Its origins remain hidden in darkness. It knows neither barriers nor frontiers. It strikes all people and religions, all political systems and social classes. Because it is willed by human beings, even God is unable to stop it. No nation is immune to its poison, no society protected from its arrows…

Hatred has no mercy for those who refuse to fight it. It kills those who do not try to disarm it.

To hate is to refuse to accept another person as a human being. To hate is to diminish a person, to limit one's own horizon by narrowing another's, to look at another person — and at one's self — not as a subject of pride but as an object of disdain and of fear…

Religious hate makes the face of God invisible. Political hate wipes out people's liberties. In science, hate inevitably puts itself at the service of death. In literature, hate distorts truth, perverts a story's meaning, hides beauty itself … If we do nothing to vanquish indifference and hate, we shall pass on to our children the message of hate under the guise of racism, fanaticism, xenophobia, and antisemitism…

Elie Wiesel
USA
1990

Kjell Magne Bondevik

Norway

The forces of hate are not far from us. Civil war is raging in Yugoslavia where ethnic conflicts have devastated the country and torn the people apart. In other parts of Europe, ethnic conflicts are also threatening peace and stability. Indeed, the world as a whole is threatened.

Once again in our century, we see racism and antisemitism disturbing civil tranquillity. In Germany, among other places, there is a revival of Nazi ideology leading to hatred and violence. In the Middle East, despite the on-going peace negotiations, violence continues, affecting children and young people especially. On the Indian sub-continent, there is a recurrence of ethnic conflict. In various parts of Africa, there are ethnic and cultural conflicts, some of which have led to bloodbaths.

The most intractable conflicts, the ones that seem impossible to solve, however, are the local conflicts, like the one in Northern Ireland. Many more occur throughout the world. Still, we must not lose hope. We must have confidence that on-going negotiations continuing in various parts of the world will have a positive effect.

What is the origin of the dark forces that cause us daily to inflict untold pain and suffering on our fellow human beings? What is the origin of the forces that create barriers against peace and justice, against cooperation and development? What is the origin of the terrible forces that at their worst, and if unleashed, could exterminate humankind?

In biblical terms it all began when Cain killed Abel. The unruly strength of hatred was unleashed, and humanity has suffered ever since. While I do not believe religion is, or ever should be considered, a facile solution for dealing with hatred, I do believe our religious traditions have something to teach us about forgiveness and love. In trying to counter hate, let us not ignore those teachings which challenge us to live together as good and decent human beings.

At the same time, if we want to find a way to live beyond hate, we must examine the anatomy of hate, and in order to do that we must delve into the inner-most workings of the human mind and heart. Only if we understand the anatomy of hate — the texture, the feel,

4

the many disguises hatred wears: bigotry, discrimination, injustice, and so on — will we be able to counter the infestation of hatred in the hearts and minds of people.

Countries and regions do not hate. People hate. In considering the global dimensions of hatred, we must not forget that our world is made up of people, of individuals. Trying to move beyond hate necessitates a change of heart. Unless the hearts and minds of individuals are changed, it will be impossible to achieve understanding and solidarity among peoples. Whatever the global dimensions of hatred, they cannot be separated from individuals or from individual responsibility. Trying to counter hatred in its many guises requires that we start with ourselves, with our relationship to other people, to our neighbour, whether at our doorstep or thousands of miles away.

At the same time, we must engage in political action aimed at changing the unjust structures, whether those be employment structures, educational structures, or structures that enable racial, sexual, or religious discrimination. But to engage in such political action, there must be a willingness on the part of people to forgive each other their wrongs.

History has taught us a great deal about how we protect ourselves from the excesses of hatred. Three methods in particular seem to have been effective over the years: alliances, regional and global organisations, and negotiations.

Our efforts to counter hatred, intolerance, and indifference must continue simultaneously at individual and structural levels. We must try to influence for good the minds and hearts of individual people through dialogue and confidence-building. These efforts must be reinforced by our efforts to create just structures in society to support the on-going work of negotiations in the human community. Only then will we have a chance to negate the terrible consequences of the tremendous conflicts facing humankind today.

I believe that fear is at the root of hatred, as I believe fear is at the root of many of our problems: economic, social, human, and political.

**James Mehaffey
Northern Ireland**

I have seen hate born of fear, hate speaking in the name of God and truth, hate holding up a distorting mirror to fellow human beings. I have seen, too, that hatred is easier learned than relinquished. Still, by looking at hatred honestly, by thinking and talking about it, and sometimes just by acknowledging our capacity for it, we open the possibility of a moral response, a first small gesture towards seeing in others not the stranger, not the enemy, but simply another human being.

**Bill Moyers
USA**

Richard Needham

Great Britain

Richard Needham

Until about 1990, ethnic division in Europe seemed to be a problem of the past. There were the problems of Ulster and the problems of the Basque, but these were rooted in the mists of past history, had gone on forever, and seemed likely to go on forever. It seemed that the rest of Europe had learned the horrific, horrible, and tragic lessons of two world wars. Then Stalin's iron curtain of terror lifted in the East, and with all the impact of tons of Czech-made semtex, the simmering ethnic distrust held back only by Soviet tanks exploded.

Latvia, Lithuania, Estonia — countries colonised by Russians since 1945 — wanted Russia out, wanted Russians out. Moldavia, the central part of Romania, followed them. Turks in Bulgaria no longer were prepared to have their language, their names, their identities wiped out by the same ruthlessness used by the Japanese to eradicate Korea's cultural and national identity after the colonisation of 1910. The Czechs and the Slovaks wanted no more of each other. The Hungarians in Transylvania, one-third of whom as the result of the 1921 Treaty of Versailles found themselves outside their borders, wanted to return to Hungary. The Serbs in East Germany became restless, as did the Ukrainians in Poland, who themselves had been forcefully resettled after 1945. There also were the Germans, the Gypsies of Romania, and the Jews of Russia. High on the European list of ethnic division is Yugoslavia: six countries and fourteen nationalities, each boiling with religious, racial, social, and economic resentments. Albanians in Kosovar, Serbs in Sarajevo, Greeks, Turks — the European list now seems endless.

The end of the Soviet Union lifted the lid on forty years of ethnic semi-peace in Eastern Europe to reveal all the horrors and tensions of the past. Why? Partly because discrimination under communism was no less blatant than discrimination in many countries with a vestige of democratic respectability, such as South Africa.

What can we do? What should we consider doing about these appalling divisions that have burst in on what was or had become an unsuspecting world? What are the practical steps governments should take? What systems of cooperation should be adopted between countries, governments, and communities to achieve a world beyond hate? Do we have the political will to do it?

Lilia Cherkasskaya

Russia

A few years ago those of us who lived in the Soviet Union could not have imagined the possibility of disorder and confrontation, of differences turning into open armed conflict on national, ethnic, religious grounds within the territory of the former Soviet Union. It has happened, however. Sporadic disorders have become organised violence which has degenerated into a total lack of restraint on the part of fighters. Killing civilians, torture, and destruction have become commonplace in these conflicts.

What lies at the root of these conflicts? Some possible reasons are the economic and social problems after the break-up of the Soviet Union. We also have experienced uncertainty, fear, and suspicion of 'the other'. People are searching for a common enemy who can be made responsible for all the ills, all the negative things in our lives. If such an enemy could be found, some people believe, all our problems would be solved. This is a myth.

How can we solve this problem? It is not an easy task. Certainly we need time, much time. We need time to teach people to be tolerant and live with differences. It is our most important task. What we must search for and find is some point where people with divergent views and beliefs can meet without having to compromise their most intimate and treasured beliefs. Despite the difficulties, I believe that solutions exist and that we shall find them, although it will not be easy.

Hate is the witches' cauldron, the witches' brew. It is a product of the strongest and most primitive of all human emotions: the will to survive. If we are to get beyond hate, we must first taste it, feel its heat, recognise its call, smell its aroma of death. And, most importantly, we must step inside it, examine its ingredients, analyse its complexities, acknowledge that it is our own imperfections that have created hate.

How can we free ourselves from the chains of hate, chains forged in the certainty of our own particular cause? Do we have the courage to confront and examine our deepest convictions, the causes we hold so tightly and espouse so vehemently? Can we challenge our certainty, expose it to the scrutiny of our peers? Can we risk the demise of our own certainty?

Paddy Doherty
Northern Ireland

Mary Robinson

Republic of Ireland

I could not have held the office of President of the Republic of Ireland for these past years without being aware of how important emblems and symbols are in a society. They have immense power that is beyond reason, beyond logic. I have seen how a modest emblem, such as a light in the window, has begun to forge an imaginative link with the extended Irish family around the world. But if symbols play a part in communication, they also can play a part in its breakdown.

Violence affects many languages. Not just the language we speak. Not just the names children call each other, the rhymes they recite, the slogans with which they hurt each other, the graffiti. Those are forms of division which are easily recognised. There are other forms of division where enormous and constant damage is inflicted by violence on our everyday language. I am thinking of images. I am thinking of the impact of television and radio in our own homes.

This damaged language which we use is made up partly of the power of symbols and images, and partly of our ability to protect ourselves from such things. The ways we have of communicating with each other have enormous complicity in fostering hatred and division.

I am not blaming television or the media. Not at all. But I do suggest we have a complex interaction with images of hatred and division. Just as they are edited by economic necessity, so we are edited by them. We become onlookers, not participants. But participants are what we need to be.

In order for hatred to thrive, imagination must be quelled, because imagination is the enemy of hatred. The 'Fifth Province' is another word for an ancient Irish imagination. Modern Ireland is made up of four provinces, yet the Irish word for province is *coiced* (meaning 'a fifth'). The Fifth Province is that free space of the imagination where we can identify with 'the other', a place which transcends the division into four provinces. It is an imaginative space wherein people can talk to one another, can move beyond hatred to imagination.

Peace, requires the development of a climate of justice and tolerance, where diversity can be accommodated, where minds are open — that Fifth Province — where change and

---

The power of narrative imagination, that is, to tell and listen to the story of 'the other', is crucial. If you are asked who you are, your best answer is to tell your story, not just to give your name or where you were born, but to tell your story. That tells the other person who you are, and their story tells you who they are. By listening to and exchanging stories with other people, one enters into empathic imagination. In terms of challenging hatred, empathic imagination is central.

Richard Kearney
Republic of Ireland

8

development are seen not as threats, but as sources of potential. It should — indeed it must — be possible to harmonise loyalty to a particular group with a tolerance of diversity, a tolerance of the values and traditions of other groups who share the same or neighbouring space.

History must not be a shackle. Rather, it should be a liberating factor, a source of imaginative insights. I believe there is in Ireland an increasing awareness of the importance of being a nation which has learned from history, but is not limited by it. Similarly, there is a strong wish to define our role in the world at a time of historic global power shifts and redefinitions by reconciling the values of nationalism and internationalism in a way which emphasises cooperation and conciliation and, in the most fundamental sense, looks to a national and world order beyond hate.

There are no longer any faraway countries of whose people we know nothing. The challenges we face are how to elaborate a clear-headed analysis of the problems of living with differences, and how to devise constructive strategies to accommodate them.

These are not tidy or reasonable matters. They are surrounded by human passion, by the untidiness of grief and anger, and by the horror of events. But in that untidiness is the humanity from which a sharing can come.

There is a powerful and poignant statement of this by John Hewitt in a poem called *The scar*. It conveys the force of a random act of humanity out of which new understandings come. Hewitt tells the story of his great-grandmother who opened her window to help a famine victim during the Famine of 1847. As a result, she contacted typhus and died. In that suffering, Hewitt found an emblem of the shared suffering out of which imaginative understanding often comes.

> There's not a chance now that I might recover
> one syllable of what that sick man said,
> tapping upon my great-grandmother's shutter,
> and begging, I was told, a piece of bread;
> for on his tainted breath there hung infection
> rank from the cabins of the stricken west,
> the spores from black potato-stalks, the spittle
> mottled with poison in his rattling chest;
> but she who, by her nature, quickly answered,
> accepted in return the famine-fever;

During my experience of captivity, I had to sit alone for four years, and every symbol I had, my clothing, my watch, my wedding ring, all my personal possessions, were taken from me. For four years, I had no freedom of choice. I had to face myself as a naked human being. I had to face the fact that conflict, anger, and hate, as well as love, were present and active in me. There was no hiding behind any symbol, no hiding behind any stereotype. I had to hold on to the only thing I could hold on to: the belief that light is ultimately stronger than darkness. I often think of that battle, of the fact that self-discovery is made painfully and slowly.

Terry Waite
Great Britain

and that chance meeting, that brief confrontation,
conscribed me of the Irishry for ever.

Though much I cherish lies outside their vision,
and much they prize I have no claim to share,
yet in that woman's death I found my nation;
the old wound aches and shews its fellow scar.

Scars are part of the cost of moving beyond hate, a movement which cannot be achieved without risks. All of us need such courage and vision.

Mary Robinson and Carol Rittner

JOHN K. ROTH

About twenty years ago, I read Elie Wiesel's first book, *Night*. It is a memoir about his experience as a teenager in Auschwitz. He begins his story by talking about a teacher he had before his family was deported from their home in Hungary. The teacher's name was Moshé. On one occasion, Elie asked Moshé a question: "Why do you pray?" Moshé thought for a while, then answered, "I pray to the God within me that He will give me the strength to ask Him the right questions."

Wiesel puts the encounter with his teacher at the very beginning of his first book. It is a theme that runs through all his writings. He takes questions to be important. Why? Because he has come to understand that human beings are likely to do harm to one another when they stop asking questions, when they feel certain, when they think they know the truth, and when they are convinced that their way is the right way and somebody else's is the wrong way. If people ask questions, particularly the question, 'Why?' Wiesel suggests it can open us to each other. It can lead us to think before we act. It can lead us to develop a kind of care and concern that might otherwise be missing.

My study of the Holocaust leads me to believe that what went wrong when Nazi Germany targeted the Jews for annihilation was that the German regime under Hitler thought it knew all the answers. It did not ask very many questions. It was sure it knew who was to live and who was to die. It was sure that Christianity was better than Judaism. It was sure about a lot of things, and the net result was that a lot of suffering and death occurred. If people had asked more questions, perhaps the situation might have been very different. Maybe our own situations can be very different, if we discover the importance of questions.

The second thing Wiesel taught me is the power of stories. He thinks that if people can share the stories of their own lives with each other, it could become the basis on which friendships are made. If we are willing to open ourselves to each other, to share the narratives of our experiences, painful as they sometimes are, but also joyful on occasion, there is a chance for sharing that can build friendship and relationships.

In his novel, *The Oath*, Wiesel tells the story of a young man who thinks his life is not very meaningful, that he does not have much of a future, that there is not much hope for him. As

It is dangerous to hate, not only for the hated — we know that the hated suffer — humankind has experienced it more than can be described. But hatred also is dangerous for those who hate, because it penetrates body and mind, like a malign tumour which grows without control, intoxicating and finally dominating and destroying the total organism. Hatred nourishes itself by further hatred, and always finds new victims. It is, as a rule, a protection against one's own anxiety, insufficiency, dissatisfaction, feeling of insecurity and guilt. These negative feelings of discontent and fear are never understood, nor recognized by the person hating and, therefore, are dangerous for the individual — and the whole of society.

Leo Eitinger
Norway

the story unfolds, he is contemplating suicide. He meets an older man who senses that he is filled with despair. The older man begins to sense that this boy might take his own life, and he decides to do something because he does not want a life to be wasted. He tries to figure out how he could enter the younger man's life in a way that might prevent him from doing something horribly wasteful. What he does is tell the young man his own story, a story about survival during the Holocaust, a story about how he tried to move beyond the devastation and destruction that he had experienced and make something good.

As the novel unfolds, fiction and reality correspond. The telling of the story by the older man to the younger man has an effect. The younger man, speaking about his older friend, says, "By allowing me to enter his life, he gave meaning to mine." That is the lesson Wiesel wants to drive home: if we share our stories with each other, we may give each others' lives meaning in unexpected — even surprising — ways. But it requires honesty, courage, even some risk taking. The result may be friendship, and for Elie Wiesel, nothing is more important than friendship.

A third thing I learned from Elie Wiesel is the urgency of protest. Questions are very important, but as we question, we may also discover that there are things that need to be changed, things that are not right, things that ought to be different than they are. For Wiesel, 'protest' should be directed against what he calls 'indifference', because, as he puts it, "Indifference to evil is worse than evil."

Another thing Elie Wiesel taught me is the significance of memory. He comes from the Jewish tradition, a tradition which emphasises memory. "If we stop remembering," Wiesel says, "we stop being." That is how important memory is: If we stop remembering, we stop existing. Questions about memory are many, and they have to do particularly with what we remember, how we remember, what we do with what we remember, whether we turn memory into something that hurts or into something that heals.

We know from our own experiences that memory is potent. It can lead to hurt and to harm, but it also can lead to reconciliation. Wiesel often suggests that one of the things we have to learn is how to use memory against itself, how to turn memory into something that can be good, something that can heal. He is an example of a person who has used his own memory in that way. He took his memory of the Holocaust and turned it into a series of projects aimed at moving people beyond hate. He used memory against itself. He experienced hate, experienced what hate can do, and his memory of that experience was precisely what led him to believe that the important thing is not to perpetuate hate but to try to move beyond it.

I spent a long time in prison and wasted away the most productive years of my life. I was in a White man's jail in South Africa. The world outside has very little opportunity to know what goes on behind those walls. When you are jailed in a

Elie Wiesel also often makes the point that we do not exist in an abstract way as human beings. We exist as particular people in particular times and places, with particular histories, particular traditions, particular experiences. What Wiesel believes is that those are the resources, the opportunities we have that enable us to reach out to other people who also are particular people, with particular histories and particular traditions. It is through our particularity that we can reach out in friendship to one another.

For Wiesel, all of the above can be summed up in the Hebrew words, *tikkun olam* — 'mending the world'. The circumstances we are in, difficult though they may be, are full of opportunity. We can make some progress toward 'mending the world' if we remember the importance of questions, the power of stories, the urgency of protest, and the significance of memory.

situation where a White minority retains its authority through brutal measures, as is the case in South Africa, that brutality becomes naked behind prison walls. Those conditions would make any man very bitter and his heart full of hate. But whether or not you become bitter or filled with hate depends on what programme, what agenda, you give yourself.

Our first preoccupation in prison was to make sure that the ideas for which we were jailed — equality, a non-racial state, pluralism, democracy, and so on — should remain alive amongst the prison population themselves. Now once you have such a constructive programme you have little room for hate in your heart.

You must understand that the warders who worked with us are themselves workers, are themselves human beings with problems who also are exploited, victims of the system. One of our objectives was to ensure that we improved relations between ourselves and these warders, that we helped them with their own problems. In that way, you forget about anything that is negative, like hate. You are dealing with human beings. You want to live in peace with these people. You want them to go and spread the same message to their own people that we want to spread to our own people. In that kind of a situation, it is very difficult to find room for hatred in your heart.

Nelson Mandela
South Africa

13

Mwalimu Musheshe and Bryn Wolfe

Telling The Story

Terry Anderson

USA

Hate? My nose was rubbed in hate for seven long years. How easy, how necessary it was to hate the people who hurt us, humiliated us, chained us to a wall. Hardest of all, they hurt the people we loved at home. And there was absolutely nothing I could do about it. Nothing I could do to remove the chains.

They gave me my water, my food, such books as I was allowed to have. Everyday they led me blindfolded to the toilet. Some of them were abusive, cruel, probably psychotic. Even the ones I thought were kind or sympathetic continued to chain me to the wall every day. It was a time that justified hate, and for a time I hated them furiously.

I was, and am, a Catholic, a Christian. I know about "love your enemy... turn the other cheek," and the rest, but the pain, the anger overwhelmed my faith, my belief. Overwhelmed me. Yet, I had to deal with those men everyday. I was totally dependent on them.

Over the long months, we began to talk to them about ourselves, about them, about their country, about ours, about our religions. And after a while they became people, individuals to me. Some of them were bad. But still, they were people, they could be understood. It does not mean I accepted what they were or their logic, just that I tried to understand them.

When you have nothing but a blank wall to look at, you start to probe yourself, to go inside your head, to look round, and to examine your motives and actions. You begin to understand your own anger, your own fear, to move through it and beyond it to a place where it begins to lose some of its power. And that, I think, is when the healing begins, when you can begin moving 'beyond hate'.

It is hard. It takes a very long time. It is not something you just do once, and it is done, finished. It is a process, not a place. For me, the process will go on for the rest of my life. At least, I hope it will.

My experience, of course, is just my own, but one thing I have learned: if I am in confrontation with another person, another group, I cannot first ask anything of the other side, even if I feel I am the victim. I have to take the first step to say, "I forgive."

It is my experience that hatred is never the first step on a journey. It usually comes at the end of a very long process. It comes when people feel and experience deep hurt again and again, when they feel threatened and exploited, when they feel helpless and victims of injustice. And above all, hatred comes when people feel that nobody cares for them, that nobody will listen to their cry. It comes when attempts are made to justify the unjustifiable.

Hatred is almost always born out of frustration and helplessness. It is a lethal and destructive phenomenon, but, in the final analysis, it is never as powerful as tolerance, understanding, and love.

Edward Daly
Northern Ireland

Written in Captivity

Satan is a name we use
for darkness in the world.
A goat on which we load
our most horrific sins
to carry off our guilt.
But all the evil I have seen
was done by human beings.

It is not a dark angel
who rigs a car into a bomb,
or steals money meant for others' food.
And it was not an alien spirit
that chained me to this wall.

One of those who kidnapped me
said once: "No man believes he's evil."
A penetrating and subtle thought
in these circumstances, and from him.
And that is the mystery:
he's not stupid, and does not seem insane.
He knows I've done no harm to him or his.
He's looked into my face
each day for years, and
heard me crying in the night.
Still he daily checks my chain,
makes sure my blindfold is secure,
and kneels outside my cell
and prays to Allah, merciful, compassionate.

I know too well the darker urges in myself,
the violence and selfishness.
I've seen little in him I can not recognize.
I also know my mind would shatter,
my soul would die if I did the things he does.
I'm tempted to believe there really is

a devil in him, some malevolent,
independent force that makes him
less or other than a man.

That is too easy, too dangerous an answer,
it is how so many evils come to be.
I must reject, abhor, fight against
these acts, and acknowledge that
they are not inhuman — just the opposite.
We can not separate the things
we do from what we are.
Hate the sin and love the sinner is not
a concept I'll ever really understand.

I'll never love him — I'm not Christ.
But I'll try to achieve forgiveness
because I know that in the end,
as always, Christ was right.

Terry Anderson

LAWRENCE JENCO

USA

The morning I was kidnapped I was wearing a cross and chain I had been given as a gift on the anniversary of my twenty-fifth year as a priest. My kidnappers spotted that cross and chain and took it away from me. When they threw me in the trunk of a car, I kept thinking, "They've kidnapped the wrong person. They'll let me go." That afternoon, I looked into the hate-filled eyes of a man who said "You are dead." For nineteen months, a gentle God said to me, "Now you must accept a different type of a cross."

I was kept in many different places. I lived on the floor, chained to a radiator. I ate when they fed me, went to the toilet when they allowed me to go to the toilet. I began to have a sense of being a little puppy dog. I found myself reminding God, "Listen, I am not a dog. I am a person of worth. I am loved. I am redeemed, I have a destiny." For six months, I was forced to remain silent because no one would talk to me. I cried, I sang *Over the Rainbow*, I complained to God. I said, "I'm not Job. I want to go home now."

"How did you cope?" people have asked me. It was not easy. The nourishments were God's word in the Hebrew and Christian covenants. I tried to recall what Jesus had said about love, compassion, gentleness, forgiveness. I would take a piece of Arabic bread and celebrate Eucharist. These two nourishments kept me going.

Sometimes I would just lie there and try to look into my mother's eyes, into the eyes of Jesus. Terry [Anderson] used to crochet rosaries. We prayed those rosaries.

One Christmas when we were supposed to go home, Terry [Waite] was on a BBC news broadcast saying he had not succeeded in securing our release and was going back to England. That night was a difficult Midnight Mass for us. But the next day, they [our kidnappers] made a beautiful cake for us. On the cake, they wrote, "Happy Birthday, Jesus." They sang to us and allowed us to write a letter to our families.

I simply wrote to my brothers and sisters, "If I'm to die, I hope that I could die with the words of Jesus on my lips, 'Father forgive them, for they know not what they do'. Please do not hate them. If you want to know how I am spiritually, read psalms 116, 117 and 118." The letter was never sent.

It is important to remember that not all hostages are chained within rooms. A lot of us are chained within our mythologies, within our history, within our fears, within our feelings of insecurity. And those chains, too, must be loosened.

Edward Daly
Northern Ireland

19

One night, a few months before my release, Sa'id, one of my guards who had been very cruel to me, sat next to me and said, "Abouna," — in the beginning my name was Jenco, then Lawrence, then all of a sudden 'Abouna' [dear father] — do you remember those first six months?" They were a horrendous six months. I said, "Yes, Sa'id, with tremendous sadness and grief for what you did to me and to my brothers." And he asked, "Abouna, do you forgive me?"

Those are startling words. I leaned against the wall and said, "Oh, Sa'id, allow me to tell you something. Sa'id, I hated you. I need to ask God's forgiveness for hating you, Sa'id. I need to ask your forgiveness, too." At that moment I knew I was free.

A few days before my release, as I was waiting, blindfolded, and uncertain what would happen, another young guard came up behind me. I knew his voice. He was the one who had blurted out to me in his passionate bitterness, "You're a dead man." He said, "Here, Abouna," and he handed me a cross. And he put his hands on my shoulders and gently massaged them. I wished I could have lifted my blindfold and looked into his eyes. I do not think I would have found a look of hate.

People who hide their faces, terrorists who refuse to look at the faces of the people they are killing, are faceless, and their victims are faceless. What makes hatred possible is that one does not look at another person's face, does not look at her reality, does not imagine the life of that person. Thus, one can kill, but if one could imagine what it is like to be 'the other' person, then it would be almost impossible to kill, unless it were a form of suicide.

As people are invited to imagine what it is like to be the other, they put down their arms. It is just not possible to continue. The possibility of caring is the possibility of imagining what it is like to be another, and the possibility of imagining what it is like to be another is the impossibility of murder.

Richard Kearney
Republic of Ireland

Maurice Bolton and Lawrence Jenco

David Kwang-sun Suh

Republic of Korea

Korea is a small peninsula sticking out of the eastern part of China, pointing toward the islands of Japan. We are surrounded by giant nations like China, Japan and Russia. For more than four thousand years of Chinese domination and Japanese invasions, we Korean people struggled to maintain our national identity. You may not be able to distinguish Koreans from Chinese or Japanese, but we speak different languages, have different alphabets, and similar, though distinctive, cultural identities.

Until the outside world knocked on our firmly closed door in the 1880s, Korea was known as the 'land of morning calm'. Koreans were sleepily enjoying 'the morning calm' when the Japanese chased the Chinese from our peninsula in 1895 and the Russians in 1905, only to swallow up our whole country by 1910.

The Japanese ruled Korea with an iron hand. They tried their best to wipe out our cultural identity. They forced us Koreans to speak Japanese in our schools, churches, and daily life. They forced us to give up our Korean names and take Japanese names. My father, a Presbyterian minister, resisted changing our family names, but after several days of imprisonment he was forced to give in. To this day I am ashamed to mention that I have a Japanese family name.

I was born in an 'age of hate', and I grew up in a 'culture of hate'. I learned it was Korean to hate the Japanese because of their brutality and violation of our human rights. We hated our Japanese school teachers because they beat us when they discovered us speaking Korean rather than Japanese. We hated them because they would not let us learn Korean history, sing Korean folk songs, or read Korean literature. We hated them because they forced us Christians to respect and pay homage to Japanese Shinto shrines. We hated them because their army forced young Koreans to fight against the Allied Forces in China and the Pacific islands during World War II. And we still hate the Japanese because of their crimes against young Korean women who were sent to the battlefields as 'comfort girls' for Japanese soldiers. To this day, Japanese school books either deny or water down the historical facts of their brutal and inhuman colonial rule over Korea during the first half of this century.

David Kwang-sun Suh

I believe in human stories, I believe in what we can share. The rest we can read in libraries.

Shulamith Katznelson
Israel

21

When Japan left Korea in 1945, after their defeat in World War II, they left a live core of hate behind. For the Koreans, Japan's loss was Korea's victory. It meant the liberation of the Korean people, but the joy of victory and liberation was short lived. Our liberation is both celebrated and bemoaned, for it reminds us that an arbitrary line was drawn through the middle of the Korean peninsula. No one was permitted to cross that line. At first we thought it was temporary. We thought Russian troops would disarm the Japanese soldiers north of the 38th parallel and American troops would disarm the Japanese troops south of the 38th parallel, but the line became an ideological wall: Russian-type communism in the North and American-type anti-communism in the South.

The wall collapsed when North Korean tanks invaded South Korea in June 1950. During three years of bloody fighting, millions of soldiers from the North and the South, thousands of American soldiers as well as soldiers from the fifteen nations under the United Nations flag, and thousands of Chinese soldiers were killed. The war, intended to help reunify Korea by force, only resulted in making the wall of division between North and South Korea higher and thicker, in separating the people more widely, and in deepening the mutual hate between the people in North and South Korea.

When the war broke out, my father, a Presbyterian minister in the North, was arrested by the Secret Police of North Korea. It was the last time we saw him alive. During the war there was a short period when the North Korean capital was occupied by South Korean and American troops. We looked and looked for my father, but we did not find him alive. I was fortunate enough to find his body. It had washed up on a river bank, tied together with five other Christian leaders, broken to pieces by machine gun bullets. I buried him on a hill overlooking the river that flows through the middle of Pyong-yang, capital city of North Korea. With millions of refugees I left the North and went South, where I joined the navy to fight against communist North Korea.

If the first half of this century in Korea was characterized by a 'culture of hate' toward the Japanese, the second half is characterized by a 'culture of hate' toward our own sisters and brothers from the North. This is the result of Korea having been divided after World War II and of the war fought between North and South Korea (1950-1953).

Division created a value system, an ideology, even a theology, of division and alienation. One was either on the ideological left or the ideological right, either on the North Korean communist side, or on the South Korean anti-communist side. One was not allowed to have doubts about one's own side or to have an open discussion about the other side's virtues and strong points. The basic value of an ideology and theology of division is hate: hateful condemnations, holy wars, crusades, purges, killing. The 'culture of hate' is a cancerous epidemic which prevents personal growth, creativity and development. The 'culture of hate' is nothing less than a 'culture of death'. It is violent and self destructive.

What did hatred do to us in Korea? It created a lack of trust in our own ability to change, personally and socially. This led to indifference, hopelessness and apathy. Hatred helped to create an environment of fear. In this environment, faith became dependency, a dependency seeking other worldly religious phenomenon. It was religion that was not for this world, for the kingdom of God, but for faith in another world. Such religious dependency led to political dependency, to dependency on super powers. One no longer trusted in God, but in nuclear weapons and in military power.

Hate also contributes to a lack of trust in one's self, which leads to a lack of trust in others. Because you do not trust others, you cannot open yourself to others. You cannot open yourself to differences, to diversity in thought, feeling, or lifestyle. You become a rigid, closed person. Once you lose trust, it becomes impossible to unite with other people. You cannot work with others, because you always suspect them. Hatred blinds us, keeps us from seeing the wider reality, impedes our thinking, prevents us from having an analytical attitude toward reality. Hatred prohibits us from having the creative energy to move beyond it.

I have been involved in the process of dialogue with North Korean Christian leaders since 1986. I confess that this has not been an easy task for me.When I met them in Geneva for the first time, I felt like one of the sons of Abel facing the sons of Cain. Instead of forgiveness, love and reconciliation, all I felt was hatred, vengeance, and revenge. I felt I was sitting next to the murderers of my father. I could not pretend by putting on a smiling face. When I went to bed, I wept through the night, covering my head under a pillow. How could I make peace with my father's killers? How could I go beyond hate? How could the sons and daughters of Abel make peace with the sons and daughters of Cain? How could I overcome a 'culture of hate'? And yet, as a Christian, I heard the voice of God calling me to make peace with my enemy before coming into the house of God, before celebrating at the table of the feast of reconciliation. This was the dilemma for me.

I recognised my brokenness, my sins against God when I recognised the 'culture of hate' deep inside my bone marrow. But, trying to overcome hate is not just my personal problem. It is our problem, the problem of our world today. Unjust structures have not yet been transformed; wrongs have not yet been corrected. The injustice of the past continues now, albeit in many different forms. In the midst of continuing evil and injustice, many of us are struggling to move beyond hate. Why? How shall we do it? What method can we use? I do

What is not beyond hate, but before hate? No child is born hating. There is a song in the American musical comedy, *South Pacific* which says it well: "You have to be taught to hate." And we are taught to hate. We educate to hatred. Those of us who are parents or grandparents know that an innocent, new-born child is devoid of hatred. Where does it come from? And what about living with our deepest differences? We always do that: we live and die with our deepest differences. How do we live in peace despite our deepest differences?

Marshall Meyer
USA

23

not have a definitive answer to these complex questions. Indeed, the questions themselves must be reflected on and responded to within different contexts.

Before we can think about strategies for getting beyond hate, we must first come together, establish connections, form community. When we create community, we forge human connections, we open ourselves to the wisdom of others. Alone, I can do little, but with others, I can struggle to overcome hatred in its many guises. In a community, we are enabled to realise the common wisdom and courage of others in the community. They can help us to distinguish between anger and hatred, to ask such questions as: What, or who, perpetuates fear and hatred? For what purpose and why? These are not questions that can be answered quickly, or once and for all. We must ponder them, discuss them, ask them over and over again.

You may be wondering if I, myself, have moved beyond hate. It is not easy for me to say "I am sorry" to my enemy brothers and sisters. Even in faith, it is not easy for me to say to God, "I am sorry" for wanting my enemies to be destroyed and punished before my eyes. It is dishonest to say that it is easy to forgive our enemies, even to ask forgiveness for longing for revenge. There is no sentimentalism here. It is not easy to accept the grace of God, to repent and confess our sins, to come to the table of the Lord in repentance, desiring reconciliation with your brothers and sisters, with God. Still, I believe we must keep trying to move beyond hate, because, based on my Christian faith, I believe it is the only way to live.

TERRY WAITE

During the first few months of my captivity, I had to endure some physical torture. The culmination of those early months came when one torturer told me, "You have five hours to live."

I said to myself, "Can this be true?" I prayed, then fell asleep from sheer exhaustion. The man returned with a companion. "Have you anything to say?" "Yes," I said, "I'd like to write some letters." "You can write one letter." "But I need to write more." "Too bad," he replied, "you can write one."

I sat facing the wall and wrote probably the most extraordinary letter I have ever written in my life to the Archbishop of Canterbury, to my wife and children, to my mother, and to a few very close friends.

I said, "I'm sorry to leave you like this. It must be very painful for you. I want you to know that I am well. I want you to try to remember that those who have killed me have done this in part because for years they have suffered misery, humiliation, disappointment, and frustration. I forgive them, and I ask that you do too."

I folded the letter and gave it to them. A man told me to stand and face the wall. I felt the cold metal of his gun at my temple. Then he said, "Another time."

Once, later, I was taken to the bathroom. I suddenly noticed that the guard had forgotten his gun and had left it right there on top of the cistern. It was fitted with a silencer.

I immediately began to picture how I could escape. It was a real possibility. But I said to myself, "If I take this gun, I have got to be prepared to use it." I realised then and there that there was no way I could kill another person. So I pulled my blindfold down, called the guard and said, "You've forgotten something."

There was another three or four years after that. They were difficult years in isolation and solitary darkness, years of loneliness and fear. God seemed far, far away. I was forced to face within myself, at the deepest level, emotions ranging from despair to hope, disappointment, irrational anger.

Terry Waite

After a long period of time I got a Bible, but reading it only made me angry. There was no consolation in it for me. In the Old Testament, I read of wars and killings, and here we were, two, three, four thousand years later, and people were still knocking hell out of each other. When I turned to the New Testament, I read about prisoners who only had to pray and the ceiling cracked, or jail doors flung open, and they were free. Believe me, no ceilings cracked, or doors opened. I kept looking for the angel, but none came. Where is comfort in all of this, I wondered.

I do not understand the mystery of how God acts, I do realise now, in a way I never did before, that there is an essential difference between true faith and magic. Perhaps, unconsciously, I was expecting magic when what was being asked of me was faith. Growing in faith through the darkness happens slowly, transformation takes place quietly, in God's time. And a deeper touch with God and with others grows. Even my mother-in-law now says that I am a bit more human! Is not that what our lives are for? To grow into our true humanity?

I am sure now that it takes no courage to put a bullet into your enemy, but it does take courage to believe that light and life are stronger than darkness, that it is essential to continue working to serve the community, all members of the community, even when the prospect for progress seems dim.

Mairead Corrigan Maguire

Northern Ireland _____

On the tenth of August, 1976, my younger sister took her three children out for a walk, and a short time later all three children were dead. I went to the hospital morgue and I saw her little daughter, Joanne, eight years of age, and her little baby brother, Andrew, only six weeks old, lying beside her. I went to the other side of the hospital to see John, aged two and a half, dying. Then, I went to intensive care, where the doctors told my brother-in-law, "Mr Maguire, your wife is dying. We do not expect her to live." Three children and my sister, either dead or dying. My sister recovered, thank God. She had two more children, but then, in January 1980, on a cold winter day, she took her own life because she could not go on.

I was once asked, "If you could meet the person or persons who did this, what would you say to them?" It is not easy to answer that question, but the day my sister's three children were buried, I went to see Mrs. Lennon, the mother of the young IRA man, Danny Lennon, who was driving the car that plowed into my sister and her three children. Danny Lennon was shot through the head by the security forces, and Mrs. Lennon was heart-broken because she had lost a son.

Danny Lennon was the product of a society in which there has not been justice, a society where young men grew up with unemployment, no dignity, and no political voice. It was a society where young men grew up with no hope. Driving a car and opening fire at soldiers was an expression of their anger.

I do not want to see any more Danny Lennons being shot in the head on my streets by soldiers. I do not want to see any more Mrs. Lennons having to suffer the death of a son at the hands of the security forces.

Anyone visiting Northern Ireland even for a short time experiences the paradox of living in this society. On the one hand, a person experiences the love of the people, their warmth and friendship, their kindness and hospitality, and on the other, one is aware that people are still killing each other after years of 'the troubles'. Why? Why this contradiction, this paradox?

Fundamental to getting beyond hate is peace. Fundamental to peace is understanding and justice. Fundamental to peace is respect for others, for their rights, their freedom of conscience. And fundamental to peace, understanding, and justice is the ability to acknowledge one's transgressions and to apologize to another person or group for those transgressions.

William J. Flynn
USA

28

We in Northern Ireland know we have to create consensus politics. We know we must learn to share and to listen to each other.

We know we are capable of doing all the things we talk about so often. We know we can write a constitution with a Bill of Rights, that we can demilitarize our society, care for our environment, feed the hungry. We are not short of people to do these things. We know we are not short of people with fine minds, dedicated people. We could write a constitution that works. We are not short of people who could solve these problems. Why are we not doing it? Where are we going wrong? What is the problem?

I believe the 'problem' is that we are human beings and that we are afraid. We are born afraid, and most of us die afraid. We are afraid to speak to one another, afraid to tell each other how we really feel, afraid to admit we need each other, afraid to acknowledge that we are capable of murder. We do not want to do that. We want to pretend that we are civilized, that we could not murder, that it is only those people 'out there', those who are 'different' from us who could murder and kill. It is the paramilitaries who do such things. We talk about them as though they are 'men from the moon' who suddenly arrive on our streets.

We are experts at scapegoating, at dehumanizing the very men and women with whom we live, with whom we have grown up. We have a habit of blaming others, not taking responsibility ourselves. We say things like, "It is the church people. If they could get their act together, we'd be all right." At other times we say, "It is the politicians. If only we had better politicians, we could get things settled." It is only when we come to realise that we ourselves are capable of hatred, of anger, of fear that we are able to move beyond hatred and begin to live with our deepest differences. The truth of the matter is we can blame someone out there, but until we begin personally to take responsibility for our own action, our own life, we are not going to get anywhere.

We know what is right and wrong, but we are afraid to act on that knowledge. We forget what we want to forget; remember what suits us. No dictator, politician or murderer ever acts on his own, not Hitler, not Saddam Hussein, not anyone. Until we take personal responsibility for our lives and for the lives of our brothers and sisters, until we get to the point of being able to say "life is sacred, all life," nothing will ever change. We will never change things. There will never be any reconciliation, much less coexistence.

I want to take responsibility. I want to say "I am sorry." I want to ask forgiveness of the young men and women in our prisons, forgiveness for not doing something before they felt compelled to take up guns, before they injured, or maimed, or killed someone, all in the

I reject the notion that 'experts' always have to be found to mediate conflicts or to advise communities about how to resolve their conflicts. I think those of us who work for organisations like the one I work for, Y Care International, have to do more to promote 'community animation'. We have to do more to encourage and enable people to recognise and use their own skills and abilities in resolving problems and conflicts. We have to acknowledge that no one from the outside is going to find a magic solution or formula. Rather, the people involved in a conflict must themselves find a way to resolve it.

Bryn Wolfe
Great Britain

For thirty years I have ministered as a Roman Catholic priest and bishop in Northern Ireland. They have been precious years for me. They have taught me so much. I have witnessed dreadful suffering and injustice inflicted on individuals and families, and I have to say that I have been constantly amazed and edified at the resilience of so many people in the face of such suffering and injustice. I am amazed at their ability to forgive and to rise above hatred. Some of these people, I can truthfully say, have taught me far more about Christianity and genuine forgiveness than I could ever have hoped to teach them.

Edward Daly
Northern Ireland

name of a United Ireland, or of keeping the North of Ireland part of the United Kingdom. I am sorry I am not more active, more passionately committed to doing positive things in our society.

I want to say "I am sorry" to the Unionists, to my brothers and sisters in the city of Londonderry, or Belfast, or wherever, here in the North of Ireland. I am sorry that I never extended my hand in friendship, that I have not made enough of an attempt to understand them, that I have not worked passionately to uphold what they hold dear that is good in their hearts. I am sorry that as a Christian woman I have never made a serious effort to build real friendships, to bring down the barriers of hatred, disgust, and distrust that exists between us.

There are no innocent people in Northern Ireland. We are all guilty. We all must say, "I'm sorry." In the Christian gospel, Jesus tells a story in which he says, if you come to the altar to make your offering to God and you recognise your brother or sister has something against you, leave your offering at the altar. Go out to your brother or sister and be reconciled. Then, come back and offer your gift to God. [MT 5:23-24]

Each one of us has a responsibility to go out to our brother or sister and be reconciled. That demands dialogue based on respect for each other, for everyone across the whole of our society, Catholic and Protestant. That is the challenge we in Northern Ireland face if we are to move beyond hate and learn how to live with our deepest differences.

DESMOND TUTU

At the height of apartheid in South Africa, I went with some Church leaders to a village about seventy miles west of Johannesburg. We went there at a time when the South African government was carrying out brutal measures, forcibly removing Black people from their ancestral homes. The particular village we visited was to be demolished, and we Church leaders, together with others, had to come to keep a vigil with the people on the eve of the first removals.

As we were praying, an old man who was a member of the village prayed a prayer that simply amazed me. This man, whose home and village shops, clinics, and schools were going to be razed to the ground, whose family and household effects were going to be dumped, probably at gunpoint in a spot where neither he nor his fellow villagers would ever want to go, stood up and prayed, "God, thank you for loving us." Here was a man who was neither literate nor educated, a man who had every right to be consumed with anger, bitterness, and hatred praying a prayer of gratitude. Why? How was this possible? From where did he get the strength?

I know another man who has been harassed by the South African police, a man who had himself along with his wife been banned, who had been in and out of prison, who said to me one day, "You know, Father, when they torture you, you look at them and say to yourself, 'These people are also God's children'. They have lost their humanity, and we must help them to recover it'." How, I asked myself, was it possible for this man, after such suffering, to say such things?

I am reminded of another man from South Africa: Nelson Mandela. People from all over the world saw Nelson Mandela come out of prison after spending more than a quarter of a century behind bars. Yet, he was not consumed with bitterness. Indeed, he possessed an incredible magnanimity. He was a man who was ready to forgive. How was it possible?

Who would have thought when Zimbabwe achieved independence, after a brutal, bruising bush war, that Ian Smith, who had imprisoned Robert Mugabe, would remain a member of Parliament, resigning voluntarily years later? Who would have thought that Robert Mugabe, after a resounding victory at the election poles, would say that the policy of his country would be reconciliation, reconstruction, and rehabilitation?

A few months ago, Church leaders took me to a meeting they had requested with President F.W. De Klerk. The purpose of the meeting was to discuss the violent conflict in South Africa and to challenge the government regarding its responsibilities for the present situation. During that meeting, Mr. De Klerk made me exceedingly angry.

For one thing, he talked for fifty minutes straight. For another, he said things like "Stop raking up things from the past that happened under a different dispensation and during a time of war." What made me angry was that he was talking about things that happened while he was a member of the Cabinet of the Government of South Africa, which was not so long

31

ago. Then, he made a joke about the migrant worker hostels erected during apartheid. These hostels have often been at the centre of violent conflict. In discussing how to handle the problem of the hostels, Mr. De Klerk said, "I do not suppose you want me to indulge in forced removals." I was angered by the way he was taking this most serious matter.

After the meeting, both Bishop Tutu and Frank Chikane told me that I must learn "to guard my face." They said that everybody in the room could see how angry I was and that I must stop carrying around so much baggage from my past. I was astonished by their remarks. These were men who had suffered a great deal under apartheid. Bishop Tutu, whose citizenship had been taken away from him, was turned into a foreigner in his own country. When his passport was reissued to him, it said "Citizenship Undetermined." And Frank Chikane, who had been detained for many years and tortured, told me — to whom none of those things had ever happened — the same thing.

What enabled them to develop such an attitude? Was it because of what they have suffered that they had somehow been able to develop an ability to see their oppressors as real persons, to recognise their humanity, without in any way necessarily trusting them, or even liking them?

Sheena Duncan
South Africa

32

You have every right to ask if I am idealizing such people. I can only tell you my experiences. There is no hope for any country, including South Africa, if people stubbornly cling to their hatreds, if they let them fester, or if they seek to heal hatred by revenge.

Such things are possible, I believe, when we do not pretend that wrongs are not wrongs. It is possible to live beyond hate when those who have done wrong are ready to acknowledge that they did wrong, when they can say, "Please forgive us for what we did to hurt you." It is possible to live beyond hate when those who are wronged are ready to forgive those who wronged them. Only then can we move beyond hate.

We must embrace our differences, even celebrate our diversity. We must glory in the fact that God created each of us as unique human beings. God created us different, but God did not create us for separation. God created us different that we might recognize our need for one another. We must reverence our uniqueness, reverence everything that makes us what we are: our language, our culture, our religious tradition.

I have no doubt that God's plan for our universe is that we should be members of one family — the human family. And I believe that divine project will succeed.

Martin Luther King Jr. used to say, "Where the law 'an eye for an eye' operates, you end up with blind people." There is so much suffering in this world of ours, so much anguish. We must learn to live with our differences, acknowledging that they are there, yet celebrating them. If we do not, I believe something else Martin Luther King said may become our destiny, "If we do not learn to live together as sisters and brothers, we shall die together like fools."

Our task as human beings is to bring a little comfort and compassion into this world filled with such anguish for so many people. If we do not learn to live with our differences, we shall end up destroying ourselves and God's beautiful world. Let us resolve once again to build bridges, to reach out to each other, to create a world of peace and justice for all people.

Mairead Corrigan Maguire and James Hawthorne

Pieter Dankert being interviewed.

Asking The Questions

Baljeet Mehra

Great Britain

Psychologists tell us that early environmental influences are important for the development of the individual. From experience, we know how strongly children want to identify with the caring adult figures in their little world. With the zeal of true fanatics, they want to grow up like their fathers, mothers, and teachers. The ferocity of this zeal is enormous because not only do they have to convince grown-ups of their loyalty, they also have to convince themselves of the rightness of their behavioural attitudes.

The parental dictum, "Do what I say, not what I do," never works with young children. Young children carry out in action the unverbalised, often subconscious, feelings of parents. Parents do not see, or do not wish to see, that children are sensitively attuned to them. This is so they can develop a foundation and make sense of their own newly emerging inner worlds. It is how one becomes a person, how the concept of 'me' and 'mine' provides boundaries which delineate the self and confirm links with the supportive social group to which one belongs. This interchange between the self and the group is of paramount importance. It serves as a lifeline, for just as an individual needs the group to confirm his/her own identity, the group needs the individual.

Many of the conflicts in today's world stem from fears and threats. Some of the threats are external, but many are internal, such as the threat of losing one's boundaries and, thus, one's identity. With the scientific, technological and industrial revolutions in the world today, the boundaries within groups not only have diminished, but, in some cases, have disappeared altogether. As inter-group differences become less distinct, the identity of the group itself is loosened. Consequently, the identity of the person needing group support, in order to find out who he/she is, becomes hazy.

The weapons of violence and usurpation are not new. The colonial, imperialistic empires of yesterday have changed their faces. They come in new guises. Often when there is an internal threat, a country will declare war on another country. Making war deflects the internal threat and externalizes the inner tensions. It restates one's power to affirm hazy boundaries, which in turn helps one to feel less impotent.

The spontaneous, almost unconscious response of one human being to another is that of 'empathy'. By 'empathy', I mean the ability to feel the feelings of another as if they were your own. It is a reaching forward which creates a bridge between two people and gives birth to an emotional bond. If we encourage people to reach forward, to create bridges, to practise empathy, more people would live in harmony, and we would not be able to kill one another so easily.

Before there can be destruction and killing, there first must be hatred which dehumanises 'the other', makes him/her 'the enemy'. This is so hatred can become functional and achieve its purpose. The Jew, for example, has to be made into a greedy, grubby Shylock character; the Black child has to be branded innately less intelligent than the White child; the Asian immigrant has to be stereotyped as obsequious, lazy, stupid; and the French have to be described as 'garlic eating frogs'. Whatever the labels, they serve to create barriers against empathy. They serve to put a distance between 'our group' and 'theirs'. Such labels stress differences to the point of caricature, and, in a negative way, they confirm 'our group' as distinct and separate from 'their group'. Such labels stress differences to the point of caricature.

In a situation of conflict, of war, the relationship which rightly belongs between one human being and another is transferred and begins to exist between one human being and his/her weapons. The outsider — the enemy — is no longer a fellow human being, but merely a target. Soldiers who carry their weapons with pride are convinced of the righteousness of their cause, whether it is patriotism, anti-communism, or religion. They become convinced that it is necessary to wipe out those with whom they disagree. They do not know, or have no way of knowing, that each time they destroy a human being, they are destroying a part of themselves, the part which already has been transferred and deposited into 'the other'. That is why in war soldiers and their weapons become one and end up de-humanising not only the enemy but the soldiers themselves.

Once I participated in an UNESCO project studying racial prejudice in India among Hindus and Muslims toward each other. The population, for the purpose of the study, was divided into three groups. One group had suffered as the result of racial conflict. They lost relatives and homes, and had been subjected to cruelty and torture. The second group were people who had not actually suffered themselves, but knew people who had suffered. The third group had no contact with anyone who had suffered. Whatever knowledge they had came from hearsay. I discovered there was an inverse correlation between personal experience and hate. Those who scored highest on the prejudice scale were those who experienced prejudice by identification and hearsay. Those who scored lowest were the victims, those who actually had suffered.

The destructive politics of family life are well known to all of us. It is in the family that we learn and experience love and interpersonal relationships as well as guerrilla warfare. If we can learn how to handle the terror and guerrilla warfare of our own families, I suspect that we shall be able to learn how to handle the terrorism and tyranny we all exert over others.

Garrett O'Connor
USA

In a study done in Israel on Holocaust survivors, researchers found that people who have experienced intense suffering, people who have been through hell themselves, are much more moderate in their political attitudes, and also much more hopeful about the future, than those who have only heard about such experiences.

Shlomo Breznitz
Israel

37

Ironically, it may be that direct contact with suffering enables a person to recognise in 'the other' his/her own reflection. This allows room for empathy. The human task we must embrace, if we are to move beyond hate and learn to coexist in a world of differences, is to find ways to develop empathic feelings in ourselves, in our children, and in others.

A pre-condition for justice must be truth, but how do you get to the truth when one of the most important things is the admission that 'my truth' is not 'your truth'. We are forced, scientifically and philosophically, even religiously, into a type of relativism. The real question is, what is truth?

Marshall Meyer
USA

Mwalimu Musheshe, Ephrem Rutaboba, Mrs. M. Wright, and Baljeet Mehra

Derick Wilson

I have lived in Northern Ireland all my life. Whenever I think about how our institutions could do more to end distrust, I always think about how I was brought up, and what I learned. In my tradition I learned to be polite, to avoid people from the other tradition because I was told that whenever I came into their presence I would feel uncomfortable. I also learned to remain separate. Consequently, until I was seventeen, I never learned how to deal with the emotions I felt whenever I met people different from me, until then I never learned to see them as people like myself — vulnerable and hopeful.

Whenever we become so much part of one tradition that we cannot meet each other as people, as human beings, those traditions are flawed. Those traditions are flawed because they carry apartness within them. They do not address the reality where we live: people brought up in different traditions yet sharing the one space.

As the result of my experience over the years, I would like to offer two suggestions. The first concerns contested societies. Wherever possible, we need to create communities of reconciliation — communities and groups which transcend differences, groups where people start to do small things together, where they begin to meet each other as human beings. We need such groups, where people can learn to listen, to hear each other, to trust each other. This is possible for children's groups, schools, youth groups, churches, community groups, sports groups, men's clubs, women's groups, and especially political groups.

Before 'the troubles' started, some of us were part of such efforts. What I learned from that experience was that when I took the risk of meeting people who were different from me, when I took the risk of becoming friends with them, years later, when other friends, or colleagues — from both sides — were killed, or members of their immediate families were assassinated, I was able to resist that primitive call to return to my own tribe. I was able to avoid the call of separation because the experience of belonging to a community of people who were my friends, even though some of them were different from me, was stronger. Just as I have learned that hate multiplies, so I have learned that freedom also grows.

The second suggestion also comes out of my experience in Northern Ireland. People like myself often are unable to believe those who are able to say, in a totally unexpected way, "I

We need a memory based on forgiveness, but we cannot forgive if we have forgotten. We have to cross over memories, to exchange memories with each other.

Richard Kearney
Republic of Ireland

What accounts for the optimism of people, for their belief that a conflict can be resolved without violence and killing? What is it in such a situation that makes it possible for people to think that it can be done differently than it unfortunately has been done elsewhere?

Shlomo Breznitz
Israel

39

forgive," even though their relatives have been brutally killed. However, it is important at such times for us to accept what these people have to say. I know not all people have been able to say that — and I do not want to create a myth that everyone can forgive — but my experience is that some can, and some have, and they have made a difference to others. It is also important that we support communities and organisations where people can meet each other across the traditions, important that we support those institutions that believe what such people say and hold their words as precious and significant. Why? Because in my experience, many of these same people — three, five, ten, fifteen years later — can be traced as having become founders or instigators of new expressions of community where different cultural and political outlooks are valued. While that is not the whole story in Northern Ireland, it is an important part of the story.

When I look at most of the integrated schools that have been started, or at many of the cross community programmes that have been initiated between Catholic schools and state schools, I see many of the same people involved who years earlier had experienced, in the kind of communities and institutions I just mentioned, some freedom, some trust.

Such communities, organisations, or programmes may not happen everywhere but where they have happened across the divisions in Northern Ireland, they have made a difference, and they have encouraged new relationships across differences to be formed. Relationships are institutions, too. They help to create hope, and they carry something new and positive into our society.

BRIAN KEENAN

Northern Ireland

Sometimes, we talk about conceptions of history, about our need to reassess and re-evaluate those conceptions. What I now know is that I constantly am making history. Every touch, every greeting, all my connections to people create history. Because I am a living being, I am a creator of history, and I am not permitted to be indifferent to other human beings.

At one point during my captivity, one of my captors, his hand trembling, pressed a gun hard against my blindfolded face — the hardness was a measure of his fear — and said, "There is only one life." I laughed, not hysterically, not with fear, but because without his knowing it, those words were a gift to me. I thought to myself, "Right, I'd better do as much as I can."

More than once, I was beaten by a man who was confused, disturbed, filled with anger, and unresolved anguish. After one such beating, he came and stood outside my door, looking over the grille. He was afraid to come in, but not because of what I could do to him. Something else possessed him. "Look at me. Look at me!" he screamed. I refused. Maybe it was my Irish stubbornness, but I was angry, and I was not going to take orders from anybody. "Look at me. Look at me!" he repeated over and over again, until it suddenly struck me. This was not an order. It was a plea for recognition.

Brian Keenan

Another time, in another place, I was alone with this man, but shielded from him by a curtain. We were alone in the room, with the TV on. He turned it off, and I could hear him say, "Bastard! Bastard! I kill you! I kill you!" He was imitating some appalling American TV programme, and he continued until he got just the right tone of aggression in his voice. I sat there thinking "Oh no, not again."

After a while, I heard him walking around, and then I heard him start to weep. Sometimes these men wept as they prayed — it was part of their prayer ritual — but this time it was not that kind of weeping. It grew louder, more tortured and more tormented. As he wept and cried out to Allah, I suddenly found myself wanting to reach out, take hold of him, hug him as a mother does her daughter, or a father his son. I still do not know where that feeling came from, but some days later it struck me, "If I can ever look that man in the eye, I will recognise myself," as we all do when we look another in the eyes.

Sometimes I used to argue with John McCarthy that what one human being does to another human being cannot, by the logic of language, be called 'inhuman'. Maybe language is inadequate to express what we experienced.

Above the gates of the American University in Beirut are carved the words, "To search, to seek, to find and not to yield." During those years, I had a lot of time to look into myself. I am not a religious man, in the accepted sense, but as I forgot about the 'not yielding' and began to do the 'searching', I discovered that suffering can be a great liberator. Maybe it is because in my searching I discovered the feminine part of myself, that softer part, the part that does not rush, the part that takes time to nurture and to be nurtured.

Hatred is a kind of insanity. We do not understand what is happening within us. We cannot share. We retreat, and in that retreat and isolation, we expose our needs and our faults, and we are exposed to our fears and our desires. Sometimes our desires shock us. We feel guilty. We do not want people to see us in an exposed condition. We long for acceptance; we long for companionship. When this chaos is happening, we begin to despise those who have what we have been afraid to admit we do not have. We hide ourselves behind recriminations. We blame others for our inadequacies. Hate takes hold of our heart and we are imprisoned. Going beyond hate means restoring this sense of loss. It means becoming whole, finding that quality within ourselves that reunites us with the world in which we live, move, and have our being.

Hate has its roots in feelings of alienation, despondency, confusion, and frustration. This leads to rage which leads to anger, and as a result of the impossibility of working out that bewilderment, we take refuge in hate. All these things feed off one another.

The antidote — love — is ultimately about conflict, not the absence of conflict. It must be experienced first on the deep level of what we are inside ourselves, then communicated from the centre of our existence, not from the periphery. It is a constant challenge, not something passive, not a resting place. It involves moving, growing, changing together.

How do we make it work? If I draw from my own experience, I would choose one word — discipline. You had to be very disciplined in those conditions. Otherwise, a terrible illness sets in and the mind goes off on its own weary, impersonal, lunatic path.

It is about becoming interdependent. It is about listening. It is about going beyond self-preoccupation, a futile narcissism. It is about beginning to experience the world not just through our own needs, our own concerns, but through those of other people as they are, not as we think they are, based on our fears and desires. Without that objectivity, in national terms, we create an idea of cultural superiority.

Society must be organised in such a way that a person's loving nature is not separate from his/her social existence, but becomes one with it. If it is true that love is the only sane and satisfactory answer to the problem of human existence, any society which excludes the development of love must in the long run perish, because it contradicts the very essence of what it means for us to be human beings.

When one talks of love, one meets catcalls or the silence of cynicism. Such nihilism is the unresolved despair from which the poison of hate will flower. To move beyond hate means to commit myself without guarantee. It bears no deceit, hides nothing, with constant thought and action for the object of one's concern. To move beyond hate involves a person in the social realm. There is no division between love and a commitment to one's own or to others. They exist mutually, or not at all, for it is a revolutionary love.

Lawrence Jenco, Maurice Hayes (who chaired the session), Terry Waite, Brian Keenan, and Terry Anderson.

What do we cherish? What do we care for? What are our values?

Mwalimu Musheshe
Uganda

SHEENA DUNCAN

South Africa

In South Africa, we have started talking to one another. We are engaged in the difficult and disciplined work of trying to see each other, Black and White, as the reality we are, not as the 'myths' created by the National Party. People are trying to get behind images and face one another in the complexity of their reality. Perhaps we shall never come to love our political opponents. We might not even ever be able to like them, but we must come to the point of being able to recognise them as persons.

A very important question for us in South Africa concerns whether or not there can be reconciliation without any true confession of responsibility for what was done during apartheid. The question is linked with the current debate about whether or not there should be amnesty for people who have committed violent acts in the past, either on the side of the government or in the struggle for liberation. The government suddenly has shown itself open to the idea of amnesty, and many of us fear that what they mean is blanket amnesty. We fear we shall never know who were the perpetrators of the many assassinations and other crimes that happened over past years and that are happening still.

The amnesty question is linked with the issue of confession and repentance. You cannot forgive someone unless you know who it is you are forgiving and why.

At a conference I attended in South Africa, made up mainly of lawyers, many were saying that at this stage in South Africa's history, truth is more important than justice. In their view, we must find a way for people who are guilty of crimes to be proved guilty in a public forum. Then, perhaps, it may be possible to forgive them, to grant amnesty, to achieve a future of reconciliation.

Communication between people is the only real potential for change, and the only real way to counter hate and to avoid the use of force and destruction. There is no alternative to dialogue. There is no alternative to seeking common ground. There is no alternative to speaking even to the enemy. I believe this is the essential lesson to draw from history, from human experience...

Gro Harlem Bruntland
Norway

We all recognise the importance of dialogue in every process geared towards conflict resolution. Inclusive dialogue is essential in breaking down the preconceived notions people often have of each other. Dialogue offers us an opportunity to better understand our differences, to come to terms with those differences, and to formulate options to our failed past experiences. Dialogue might even lead to peaceful coexistence.

Caoimighin O'Caolain
Republic of Ireland

Kadar Asmal

South Africa

I am a South African, born in that beautiful country, forced into exile over thirty years ago by the evil system of apartheid. I am a member of the African National Congress (ANC). When I finally was able to return to South Africa in 1990, I discovered again the humanity and generosity of the oppressed, many of whom I have worked with, most of whom have been in prison, nearly all of whom have been tortured. They are the victims of apartheid. And yet, they are the ones who have taken the first step toward ending the perpetual cycles of domination and subordination that have been the signature of apartheid. With great generosity and common sense, and with a view toward advancing security for all, they have indicated their willingness not to do to the minority what the minority have done to them. Through their organisations, the victims of apartheid have shown they are willing, indeed anxious, to live under a new constitution that guarantees equal rights to all, that prevents the subordination or harassment of anyone. The victims of apartheid want to build a new South Africa where all are valued and cherished equally. The victims of apartheid want to build a South Africa which will celebrate differences, not be threatened by them, a South Africa which will find enrichment in diversity, not be fearful of it.

I hate apartheid. I hate the exploitation. I hate the degradation. I hate the humiliation, the suffering, and the slaughter. I hate the system of apartheid that can only be maintained by monstrous evil and pain. I hate the pain inflicted on the people of South Africa. But, I do not hate Pik Botha or F.W. De Klerk, and it has never entered my consciousness to hate White South Africans.

As an elected member of the ANC's National Executive Committee, I should have taken part in the march in Boipatong (in September 1992). Instead, I was here in Derry, and I could only watch helplessly as the television cameras showed the carnage wrought by the guns of apartheid. I could only watch as those guns were fired into a crowd of peaceful, unarmed marchers asserting their right to free association and free political activity. My anger and outrage defy words.

Like so many of my generation, I have been deeply influenced by the leaders who have led the struggle against apartheid, thoughtful people like Albert Luthuli, the first Black lawyer from Africa to win the Nobel Peace Prize (1960), Oliver Tambo, and Nelson Mandela.

Kadar Asmal

It is often the case that the powerful ones, the victimizers, the oppressors, come to the oppressed, come to those who have been maimed and massacred, those who have lost loved ones, and say, "We must have a reconciliation. You begin." Such people never repent, never say, "We are sorry. We apologise for what we have done to you and your loved ones." They try to force reconciliation. This is nothing short of total injustice. Sometimes former oppressors come with money, trying to buy reconciliation. This, too, is unjust. There can be no reconciliation without genuine repentance.

In 1988, the South Korean Christian Council of Churches drafted a Declaration on Peace and the Reunification of Korea. The first thing they called for was repentance, repentance before God and before the people of Korea. South Korean Christians, they said, must repent of their failure to forgive their North Korean brothers and sisters, and they must repent of their deep-seated hatred towards communism. It was because of that public act of repentance that North Korean Christians began to talk to South Korean Christians. Repentance and forgiveness go together.

David Kwang-sun Suh
Republic of Korea

During all the years of the struggle, even when under intense pressure to do so, they never abandoned non-racial values and democratic policies. They never moved away from the tolerant, dignified, and democratic vision of the Freedom Charter of 1955. In the midst of the nightmare of two hundred Laws of Racism passed in the midst of the 'grand design' of 'cleansing' South Africa of Africans, in the midst of three and a half million Africans brutally uprooted and forced into exile in their own country, in the midst of that nightmare, they still did not abandon these fundamental values and democratic policies. Indeed, they promoted and adopted democratic structures. In the midst of the nightmare of racism, they affirmed the Freedom Charter which declares to all the world that South Africa belongs to all the people who live there, Black and White.

The Freedom Charter of 1955 is not a theoretical, academic essay on how to combat hatred. The Freedom Charter is an affirmation of humanity, a repudiation of the vision and nightmare of racism. There is no reason today, no advantage for the democratic movement, even after the carnage of Boipatong, to repudiate this golden thread of non-racialism. Only a negotiated settlement, a settlement that does not require victims, a settlement that does not require the debilitation of the vanquished can combat the evil of apartheid.

Some people, in their pain and desperation, advocate a return to the armed struggle. I do not believe we should do so, but neither do I believe we can go back to a system of negotiation where what we thought we had agreed to is constantly undermined by new conditions imposed by the government. We cannot return to a non-democratic vision of South Africa, to a South Africa that is not free, that is not based on democracy. If we are able to rebuild South Africa, we must do so to show our determination to achieve democracy for all people in South Africa, Black and White.

If we are to remove the lingering effects of apartheid, we must continue the process of negotiation. But before we can do that, we, and the many political prisoners still in jail, must see a concrete effort, initiated by the government, to stop the bloodletting that is destroying the heart of South Africa. Only then can we resume the negotiation process.

As long as the government continues to deny its responsibility for the evils of apartheid, to deny its responsibility for the sufferings and the brutal murders committed throughout the last two years, reconciliation cannot be achieved. The African National Congress has said again and again that it does not come to the negotiation table in the spirit of a victor to impose a solution. No, the ANC comes as an equal partner to the negotiations. If agreement is reached, it must be seen as an achievement for all South Africa.

We do not want experts and highly paid lawyers to draw up a constitution. Such a constitution would have neither credibility nor legitimacy. We believe that all the people of South Africa must be involved in the process of drawing up a new constitution. Only then will all the people feel they have a stake in the outcome, a responsibility for making the constitution work. A constitution is not valued for what it contains, but for the route travelled to achieve what it contains. That route must be democratic. Therefore, we want a constituent assembly. We want elections for a constituent assembly. We want an interim government based on 'power sharing' which will plan and organise elections for a constituent assembly which will work toward achieving a democratic constitution. Only then can we complete the process of negotiation and embark on the path of national healing.

The first principle of our constitution will be unique in all the world: South Africa will be a non-racial and a non-sexist state. In 1943, the victims of apartheid told Winston Churchill and Franklin Roosevelt, "We want a Bill of Rights." Today, fifty years later, we say it again, "We want a Bill of Rights," a Bill of Rights that will put rights beyond the reach of a transient majority in a government. Such a Bill of Rights will provide for the supreme law of the land. It will be part of the healing process, part of the social contract we will enter into with the oppressor, a social contract that will enshrine cultural, religious, and social rights, and most important of all, the political and civil rights of all South Africans.

We do not wish to choose between bread and freedom. We do not believe, as the poet Shelley wrote, that "freedom is bread on a comely table spread." We want to put cultural, religious, social, political and civil rights in the constitution so that we can recognize our differences, but also that they do not become the basis for oppression. We want to safeguard the rights of all so that the power of the state never again can be used against its opponents.

We are in uncharted waters. So many of the certainties of this century have crumbled or eroded. Many of the noble ideas proclaimed by earlier revolutions have failed to bear fruit and that failure has ended in turmoil, fear, and old suspicions resurfacing and reverting to narrow and exclusive ethnic and religious loyalties, if not barbarisms.

Throughout the world people continue to demand not just a decent life, but a life of dignity with justice and freedom. They want a voice in helping to shape their future. In South Africa, we believe we have a glorious opportunity to begin a process that will unite people, not divide them. We recognize the difference between nation-building in an exclusive way and nation-building in an inclusive way. 'Balkanizing' the Balkans has not brought stability to Southern Europe. We believe that 'balkanizing' South Africa will not bring peace to Southern Africa. What we need is a mutual acknowledgement of our interdependence and

Fifty-two percent of the Black population, the generation born since 1971, in South Africa is under the age of nineteen. All they have ever known is violence, death, terrible socio-economic conditions, and humiliation. The experience of violence is very real. Children going to school in the morning in Soweto, or in many parts of Natal, regularly, as a matter of course, pass a dead body on their way. This is a generation that has little education, no skills, and practically no prospects for employment. At the present time, only seven out of every one hundred new entrants into the job market can hope to find a job.

In South Africa today, there is a growing maturity in our political debate at the leadership level and I do not just mean at the level of national leadership. I mean also at the level of regional and local leadership, both in the churches and in the various political parties. My great anxiety at the moment is how to translate such an understanding of human relationships to the vast majority of young people in our country.

Sheena Duncan
South Africa

47

a shared national revulsion against violence, against oppression, and against racism. We do not want forced unity nor artificial diversity. It is only on the basis of the acceptance of the principle of unity and equality that diversity can freely express itself and not be associated with domination.

The choice in South Africa is still between good and evil, between allaying anxieties and suppressing them. The struggle for human rights and for self determination is a struggle of humanity against the misuse of power, against intolerance and hatred. It is also, as the Czech writer Milan Kundera said, the "struggle of memory against forgetting." We must ensure that the memory of apartheid, the memory of so much unnecessary suffering endured by so many people for so long is victorious, because only then will memory become a shield to protect others from suffering. Only if memory is victorious will we be able to defeat intolerance, racism, and oppression.

I do not think the notion of a quest for truth is an abstract philosophical matter.

Kadar Asmal
South Africa

The question of truth is a very difficult one, because I think it is not 'the truth' we are talking about but the label of truth. These are not the same. Our exercise is not an academic one, but a political one. What we are trying to determine is the level of truth necessary for national reconciliation. The relationship between truth and national reconciliation is not an easy one. It is a very ambiguous one because it is a politically mediated relationship.

Ruben Zamora
El Salvador

Marshall Meyer

I lived for 26 years in Buenos Aries. I fought against the fascist dictatorship of the military junta. I was appointed by President Alphonsine as the only non-Argentine on the National Commission of Disappeared Persons. We never established 'the truth'. We tried, but we never could. We took the testimonies of the parents of 'the disappeared'. We knew they had 'disappeared', but we could never establish the truth of what had happened because the torturer and the murderer never admitted their deeds. Even saying that someone 'disappeared' is ironic, because while my glasses may disappear, or my pen, a human being does not disappear. A human being is murdered. They were all murdered. Nobody 'disappeared'. Occasionally a mother or father received a few bones of a son or daughter, but they never knew what happened to end the life of their child. We never had 'the truth'.

Marshall Meyer
USA

Shulamith Katznelson talking to girls from St. Cecilia's Secondary School.

Educating Against Hate

Jimmy Carter

USA

The most pressing issue facing us today is trying to live peacefully together despite the differences that all too often succeed in tearing us apart. As increasing numbers of nations realize their autonomy, and as people seek to live together, we must find ways to get beyond ethnic, economic, cultural and religious barriers that are obstacles to peace.

How can we ever hope to get beyond hate if the only contact we have with each other is violent? Violence is not a solution. We must begin to exchange our interests, our skills, and our knowledge. We need to teach our children that difference is something to be valued, not feared, that we all have something to offer each other.

You cannot create economic opportunities for a better life in an environment of fear, distrust, and violence. War and development are mutually exclusive. In my own country over a hundred years ago, we spent four years fighting a civil war because of racial, economic, and political disparities. The consequences of that war are with us still. The southern part of the United States, including my own state of Georgia, remains less developed than the north.

From my own experience, I know only too well the difficulty of getting warring parties to sit down and talk to one another. Getting them to compromise in order to end their fighting is even more difficult. Too frequently, leaders are afraid to compromise because they fear compromise makes them appear weak. But there is no weakness when compromise results in saving lives. I know from experience that it is possible to find face-saving ways to resolve seemingly intractable conflicts.

During the Camp David talks — which resulted in the peace between Egypt and Israel — then Prime Minister Menachen Begin was unable to agree to withdraw Jewish settlers from the Sinai. He had taken an oath not to do so. Thus, we were faced with a dilemma: How to allow him to fulfill his oath, and, at the same time, how to find a solution to the issue of removing Israeli settlers from the Sinai.

A compromise was found. We reached an agreement that the Knesset — the Israeli Parliament — would first agree to the removal of the settlers from the Sinai, then Prime Minister

Begin would accept their decision. Removing the settlers was not his decision but the Knesset's decision. It was this compromise that made possible the peace treaty between Israel and Egypt.

My hope is that by the time our children and grandchildren are grown, we no longer will need to talk about resolving armed conflicts, that by the time they reach adulthood, we will be living in a world that values human difference. Those are the goals towards which we each must work if our world is to have a humane future.

Ivana Balen, Fatima Nahara, and Mai Thanh.

Radim Palous

Czech Republic

For the first time in history, we live in a common global civilisation. This togetherness affects not only humankind, but all created things: animals, plants, air, water, and nature in general. This situation has many advantages, but it also has its dangers.

We likewise live in an era of democracy. Democracy is a social arrangement in which people can make their own decisions about their fate. Like our common global civilization, however, such a situation presents both advantages and dangers. In a democracy, unlike a totalitarian system, no one person makes a definitive pronouncement for all others about truth, about faith, or about the best solution to public affairs.

The role of education in a democracy is crucial. It is the task of education to lead people from ignorance to knowledge, from a lack of understanding to understanding.

All over the world the uniqueness and individuality of peoples, regions, and nations are gradually vanishing. This creates anxiety among many people. Demagogues have a flair for 'smelling out' this often inarticulate but deeply felt distress. By cunning manipulation of this distress, they can open a door to violent conflict among peoples, regions, and nations who feel a sense of loss and confusion about their identity and place in the world.

Education has a role to play in trying to alleviate the possibility of violent conflict by cultivating two principles: the principle of individual uniqueness and authenticity, and the principle of relationship and moral conscience. Educators must seek to harmonise both principles in themselves and in their students. Their role at all levels of education is immensely important if we are to learn to live together as moral beings with our deepest differences.

Educators must help students make a 'connection with difference' by building in opportunities to address issues of cultural diversity through the sharing of personal histories and life stories. Inevitably, students will confront the question of sameness versus difference and the politics and dangers of assuming that all people should think and look alike. Alongside such opportunities to explore difference at a personal level, the standard curriculum should be designed in such a way that it incorporates major critiques by people on the margin of mainstream theory and practice. Educators should search out and include in their courses the thinking and writing of feminists, men and women of colour, people with experience and expertise in other cultures, people sensitive to issues of class.

Our task as individuals is to find a space where we and our children, our neighbours and co-workers, can find and strengthen our voices, learn to listen to the voices of others, and develop the art of 'really talking' with other people who are separated from us by gender or race, culture, religion, or partisan politics.

Nancy Goldberger
USA

54

John K. Roth

Elie Wiesel often has said, "Be careful with words, because words can kill." Memory can do the same, and so the questions of what to remember, and how, require education's attention and its revision as well. As the Canadian writer, Mary Jo Leddy comments, memories serve us well when they present us with the possibility of making choices and promises that will make a humane difference in the future. Questions about what to remember and how also lead to others, to issues about anger as well as to questions about forgiveness. The latter topic is troubling and complex, but I would like to make one comment about it. To some extent, the healing and mending of the world depend on the human capacity to repent and to forgive. I think we all know this, but it is a point we need to remember if there is to be education against hate.

We often speak about the importance of education in helping people to move beyond hate and live with differences. I think we have to be very tough-minded about the pluses and minuses that education carries with it. We should not make the mistake of thinking that we do not have to be critical about education, that it only contains hope and not reason for despair. Education itself can be part of the problem because of the diverse purposes to which it can be put.

In the United States, for example, education sometimes functioned to divide people, as when it segregated Blacks and Whites. At other times, it was used to serve the interests of the state, even when those interests are problematic, for example, when government officials argue that the reason we should support education is so that Americans can be more economically competitive in the world.

A few years ago, I participated in a conference entitled *Education Against Hate*. I want to draw attention to the word 'against' in the conference title. Early on, Elie Wiesel, who was the conference chairman, spoke about using hate against hate. During the session on religion, there also was mention of the idea of using religion against religion. Used in these ways, 'against' suggests movement, a rhythm, a way of thinking and acting that can be quite powerful.

Many history books are misleading, containing a lot of self-serving information about 'the other side'. While the information may not be false, it can give an impression of 'the other side' that is misleading, perhaps even a deliberate distortion. It is always important for people to know what they are talking about, but it is particularly important in a situation of conflict, because 'historical facts' play a more crucial role in influencing what people do than some people may think.

If, at some point, you try to resolve differences with 'the other side', you must get a glimpse into how they are portrayed in your history books as well as how you are portrayed in theirs. Overcoming deliberate distortions of history is more difficult and less tangible than overcoming ignorance.

Pieter Dankert
Netherlands

Using education against itself entails using memory against memory. Where hate is concerned, memory seems essential. It stands in opposition to one of the claims that people make from time to time, namely, that ignorance is the core of hatred. In a way, that claim is true, but only in a way, because if ignorance is fully present, I doubt that there is content to provoke hate.

Experience, more than ignorance, provokes hate. Experience, moreover, involves memory, and memory of what has happened can fuel hate. It can do this so much, in fact, that we might say, "No memory, no hate." But memory does exist, and thus, in some ways, we have to work against memory. Doing that well, however, entails remembering. Thinking and acting through our past, shared and particular, so the damage and waste of hate is at least checked is part of what is involved when Elie Wiesel states that "If we stop remembering, we stop being."

Using memory against itself so there can be education against hate entails the recognition that we need to think more about using structures against themselves. When I use the term 'structure', I have in mind elements that are many and diverse. They include, to list only a few, dimensions of human life that are political, economic, religious, cultural, journalistic, literary, and psychological. Is the most important dimension the literary, as some suggest, or the religious, as others suggest? That realization seems more important than debates about hierarchies.

Consider, for example, the political realm. On more than one occasion, I have heard people say that "democracy and hate are opposed." Perhaps they are, but only if democracy intends to be against hate. Hate, unfortunately, can thrive in democracy, too. Democracy has to work against itself to keep hate at bay. So does nationalism. So do all our hopes, ideals, and commitments.

Consider, too, the psychological realm. Dr. Nathaniel Laor, a psychiatrist from Israel, drawing on his clinical experience, says that hate damages psychic structures. If I follow him, there are two factors that play an especially crucial role in that syndrome. First, hate gives, or can give, a form of pleasure. (As the saying goes, we may "love to hate.") Second, hating is addictive. It can even become epidemic, if not endemic. While it is an idea that needs to be developed more fully, it seems to me that the syndrome of hate-pleasure and addiction-epidemic suggests elements of a conceptual framework that may have implications for education against hate.

When we think about hate and getting beyond it, we also need to be attentive to the outcomes education produces, if we are to have the kind of education that will humanize us and not simply turn us into more fierce competitors, into winners and losers, into haves and have-nots, or into killers.

One last observation: There is, I think, a challenge in the question, "Should those who seek to move beyond hate expect to be victimized by it — at least in the short run?" I am not sure I know or even want to know the answer to that question. It is a dilemma that belongs among what one might call 'the right questions'. It is a question to which we would do well to give attention.

Claire Gaudiani

USA

The most powerful element for education against hatred is literature, specifically the literature of suffering and, more specifically, the literature of suffering written by the suffering witness...

In choosing to read, we agree to make ourselves vulnerable to change, to change of mind and to change of heart.

Literature becomes a stepping stone to others... a microcosm where we can explore their lives. Literature itself provides a stepping stone from 'the self' to an encounter with 'the other', perhaps the one is potentially hateable, or already hated. It offers an interim experience in knowing. Literature can make the abstract real and personal, because it creates individual memories.

The literature of suffering dispels a reader's emotional neutrality, closes the safe distance that political, social, economic, or cultural differences design to spare us the painful details in the lives of other individuals or groups. It collapses the distance that convinces us of our uniqueness, our special worthiness. This literature yanks bitter reality out of cultural abstractions. The Jew, the Black, the Russian, the Japanese move out of general categories and become Anne Frank in hiding, the young Elie Wiesel burying his watch in the backyard, Harriet Jacobs under the front porch of a house hiding from the terrible master, the young women whose lives were transformed by an atomic bomb, a frightened prisoner in a cell in Sao Paulo, or Johannesburg, or Siberia.

Literature creates for the reader personal experiences, intimate memories that become part of his or her own time. The memory of suffering shared can overcome hatred. The experience of commonality breaks down the categories of nationality, ethnicity, race, and religion which create the differences and the distances that make hatred possible.

Wole Soyinka

Nigeria

I have often asked myself: What is the unique perspective of any nation on the reality of human pain and suffering? Is pain experienced in cultural terms? Is the Asian cry for anguish, involuntarily wrung in protest against the abuse of Asiatic flesh, any different from that of a Kenyan wallowing in his own vomit in a Kenyan prison, or any different from that of an aboriginal Indian suffering the effects of extermination in parts of South America still largely shrouded from the glare of world concerns? Must every race now present its human credentials before anyone listens to its cry of pain? Perhaps we should translate into every spoken language in our world, emphasizing their sheer ordinariness, the words of the much abused Merchant of Venice: "Hath not a Jew eyes? Hath not a Jew hands, organs, dimensions, senses, affections, passions?...If you prick us, do we not bleed? If you poison us, do we not die?"

How, I have often wondered, would those words translate into Afrikans? Would it read alien in KwaZulu? Or, perhaps most pertinently, in view of the abuses in the occupied Gaza strip, what would it sound like in Hebrew? or Arabic? To move closer to home, I picture a little scene: Daniel arap Moi and Pieter Botha seated together, listening to a simultaneous translation of these prosaic lines in their own native tongues, delivered by a representative victim from either state. Would the victims be greeted by a simultaneous guffaw, a conspiratorial wink or chuckle from their august listeners?

Throughout history, artists have expressed joy and sadness, hope and fear, memories of the past and visions of the future. Artists have been at the frontier of identifying, interpreting and reinventing their realities, both personal and political. And in a world fraught with misunderstanding, crossed purposes and conflicts, they have sought and found common ground.

When we speak of a new Europe, or even more broadly, of a new world order, we do well to look to the artist who dares to question conventional wisdom, to make order out of chaos, harmony out of discord. Artists like scientists perform miracles, if we take miracles to be the new products of human ingenuity, to be new and creative solutions to old problems.

Sondra Myers
USA

Sondra Myers and Johnny Bayless

Johnny Bayless

Roma Casey and Ali Yehie Adib

Edward Daly, Paul Arthur, and Magaret Heckler

Living With Differences

Richard Kearney

Republic of Ireland _____

All the great founding myths and narratives tell of the origins of culture in terms of the conflict between two rivals. In a sense, this is the rivalry endemic in human culture: we desire 'desire'; we desire what the other has and what we apparently cannot have.

Douglas Hyde, the first President of Ireland, said about the Irish "The English are the people we love to hate and never cease to imitate." It is such sibling rivalry which ultimately leads to conflict in society.

On the island of Ireland, there is a coveted, mutually exclusive object, called 'sovereignty'. One community wants a United Ireland, the other wants to retain a United Kingdom. Both claims for sovereignty are exclusive. The more one wants it, the more the other wants it. The more one can have it, the more the other cannot have it. This leads to a cycle of mimetic rivalry where one desire feeds off the other. It is only when both communities agree to seize sovereignty and share sovereignty that rivalry can actually be gotten beyond.

According to one theory, scapegoating was the means devised by western society to deal with rivalry and conflict. It was a way for two rival sibling communities to come together and say "Why fight with each other? Why not find somebody outside that we can agree to hate together?"

In the Middle Ages, people scapegoated persons, usually women, who practised a non-Christian way of healing. Called 'witches', they were either burned or drowned. Rather than facing the shadow within themselves, a sense of consciousness was created, a sense of communal solidarity. In sacrificing the scapegoat, people projected all their anxiety, all their unease, all the evil and violence of their society onto the scapegoat.

Scapegoating ultimately is doomed to fail, because it always is based on a lie. For example, antisemitism, which scapegoats Jews. During the Middle Ages, Jews were accused of poisoning wells, corrupting minors, and introducing licentiousness into society. None of this was true, but the Jews were different, a minority in a Christian society. Centuries later, during a time of conflict, racism, and unemployment, they were blamed for the collapse of the German economy during the Weimar Republic, accused of contaminating the 'pure'

Germanic race. Nazi Germany projected all of its inner violence and division onto the Jews. Because it was based on a lie, it was bound to fail, and it did. But, unfortunately, what we know from history is that often, when one scapegoat fails, people look for another.

Scapegoating is a perverse use of imagination because what a person is doing is projecting an image of his/her own problems, fears, anxiety and divisions onto 'the other'. That is how they serve us, by carrying our shadow for us.

Nicholas Gillet and Michael Wright enjoying a joke together.

SHEENA DUNCAN

South Africa

Over the years of apartheid in South Africa, the National Party successfully created a negative 'myth': an image of the 'enemy'. The 'enemy' was Black, communist, un-Christian, violent, terrorist, revolutionary, and uncivilised. One example of this myth-making is what they did to Archbishop Desmond Tutu. He was not part of any of the liberation movements; he was never 'banned'. Indeed, he was free to speak in public and in the media. Still, the government was able to create an image of him that was both negative and astonishingly clever.

Bishop Tutu often was on television, which is government controlled, but they always made sure that the TV lights glinted on his glasses so that you could not see his eyes. The result was that over time they subtly created an image of him as a revolutionary, a person who exemplified the 'enemy': treacherous, sneaky, hidden. The National Party also created the 'myth' of a glorious Black revolutionary liberation army which would one day come marching into Pretoria and take power by force. These negative 'myths' were entirely successful and shaped our national life during all the years of apartheid.

Another nasty 'myth' — it is one that so many people in the North [Europe and America] have accepted — is the one that describes the violent conflict in South Africa as 'Black on Black' violence. I have never heard the conflict here in Northern Ireland referred to as 'White on White' violence. What is so destructive about this myth of 'Black on Black' violence is that it prevents the possibility of analyzing what is actually happening in South Africa.

These 'myths' worked both for White people as well as for Black people. For many years, Bishop Tutu's integrity and credibility were called into question among the White majority of South Africa. He was effectively marginalized. And young Black people were especially attracted to the 'myth' of a glorious revolutionary liberation army which would take power by force in South Africa. The damage of that myth and its attraction are still with us. The myth of the revolutionary Black 'enemy', however, has ceased to exist among those involved in the ongoing negotiations.

We tend to depersonalize the objects of our hatred, even to make them sub-human. Sometimes, with proximity, the atmosphere of hatred is generic and not aimed at individuals. This is how it was with our Black neighbours in the American South. Our own friends, playmates, and working companions were very good people; it was just other Negroes, in general, who were inferior. On other occasions, we and our political leaders make every effort to personalize the hatred. We not only were taught to despise Hitler, Mussolini, and Hirohito, but we considered all Germans and Japanese to be 'Huns', 'Japs', and much worse during World War II.

Jimmy Carter
USA

Romila Thapar

India

Where communities have co-existed for over a millennium in various parts of the world and where today they are in conflict, such as Hindus and Muslims, Tamils and Sinhalas, Jews and Arabs, there the perception of the past which each has, both of itself and of the other, is crucial to understanding the dimensions of the conflict. Stereotypes, supposedly from history, intervene in contemporary relations. These are so deeply ingrained as to be almost genetic. Only a sharply self-conscious discernment can keep one from being imprisoned by stereotypes.

The consciousness of a particular kind of history becomes instrumental in both the construction of hate and the articulation of this hate in violent forms. The perception of the past is carried over into the present. It is exploited to legitimise the actions of the present. Where confrontations derive from a particular reading of history, it becomes imperative to constantly examine the motivations of these readings and to consider whether the legitimacy sought from the past is justified...

The use of religion towards political ends, by no means new in history, today requires a discussion of religious fundamentalism which, the world over, has become a powerful force, perhaps even more so than in the past. Today, attempts are being made to remould religions such as Hinduism to accommodate a fundamentalist position, in spite of the fact that traditionally it was extraneous to such religions.

Religious fundamentalism draws on religious loyalties, reiterates the notion of a single, true belief, excludes non-believers, and subordinates civil society to the laws of religion. Fundamentalism cannot be explained away merely as the wish of a society to focus on a religious identity. In our time, religious fundamentalism, be it of a Hindu, Islamic, Buddhist, Jewish or Christian variety, is built on the reality of an aggressive political mobilisation and reflects the social alienation evident within such societies...

There is no single solution to the breeding of hatred and its detonation, but possibly some awareness can be generated which might illumine the roots of hatred. Perceptions of the past, as also actions in the present, require a continuing dialogue among conflicting groups.

Michael Melchior

Norway _____

I was born in Denmark. My grandfather, originally from Denmark, was a Rabbi in Germany. In 1933, when the Nazis came to power in Germany, they closed down most of the Jewish activity there. Everybody who could be dispensed with, like my grandfather, who had Danish citizenship, was sent back to his or her country of origin. He went back to Denmark but could not get any job as a rabbi. Consequently, he travelled throughout Denmark and spoke about Judaism, but only in non-Jewish congregations, in non-religious groups and clubs. He used to say, "I want to tell you who we Jews are. I believe that by taking away the mystery around Jews and Judaism you will be able to understand us better. We are not the same as Christians. We are different. We believe different things, but we are also human beings. By taking away the mystery, the myths about the Jews, by making them human beings like yourself, I believe that we can contribute, not only to you understanding us and us understanding you, but also to all of us understanding others. Just as there are myths about the Jews, there are myths about many other groups. When you know who people really are, you see that a lot of your assumptions and ideas about others are just not true."

It was this, among other efforts, that created something great in Denmark during World War II. In October 1943, the Germans decided to arrest the Jews of Denmark, like they had everywhere else they were in control. My grandfather was tipped off by a German that they were going to take the Jews and send them to concentration camps. My grandfather warned the people at the morning service on the day before the Jewish New Year. He said, "Go home! We are cancelling the service. Go home and hide with your non-Jewish friends. Get away as soon as possible!"

The incredible thing was that not just a little group but hundreds of thousands of non-Jewish Danish people, at great danger to their lives, helped the Jews. They took risks and got the Jews to Sweden, which saved their lives. I believe that it was possible because of the effort made by my grandfather, by his hard work going out into the communities, into schools organisations, and clubs and telling non-Jews about Jews and Judaism, telling them about who we are and why we are.

Telling people who you are and why you are as you are can make a difference. It can help understanding and tolerance. In October 1943, when Danish people had to prove they were

Judging by history, with the exception of brief flickers of hope, the human capacity to tolerate misery on a universal scale has been well entrenched for some time. The story of humankind can be easily measured by yardsticks of human-made disasters. But even when fully told, when not a single terrible item is left out, the Holocaust stands out as a unique horror, unparalleled by any other. And yet, the single most important condition for enabling the Holocaust to happen was the indifference of millions who were only marginally touched by the terrible virus that devoured all of continental Europe. Hate? Yes. There was a cataclysmic release of hate which fuelled the monstrosity.

not indifferent to other people's suffering, they reacted like they reacted, not like what happened in most other places in Europe where people closed their eyes and the Jews were sent to death.

In Babi Yar, for example, tens of thousands of Jews were killed. The incredible thing is that I always believed that Babi Yar was somewhere out in the forest. The truth is that Babi Yar is part of the city of Kiev. Everyday people saw the Jews going through the streets, yet there is not one case recorded of one person stretching out a hand and helping a Jew. Education, caring, involvement makes a difference.

The greatest threat to society is not the haters. The greatest threat is the people who do not care, who believe that nothing can be done, who despair, who say that the task is just beyond them. If there is anything we learn in religious studies, it is that every single effort helps. There is a Jewish saying, "If you save one person's life, you have saved the whole world." If you stop one person from suffering, you have stopped the whole world from suffering. Helping one person is within the possibility of every human being.

Yom Kippur, the Day of Atonement, is the holiest day in the Jewish calendar. It is a very serious day. We fast, we do not eat and we do not drink. We do not do anything else but pray for twenty-five hours. We have a little sleep in the middle of the day and then we go back to the synagogue and pray. It is a day when nearly the whole Jewish people, even those who never come to synagogue, come. It is a day to ask forgiveness from God and from your fellow human beings. It is a day of self-search, a day to go into yourself, to see how you can become a better human being. A man with a big smile on his face came to greet his rabbi after such a day. The rabbi wondered, why is this man coming with such a big smile? True, we believe in the power of forgiveness and atonement, but why such a big smile?

The man said, "I know, I am sure, I am positive that God has forgiven me my sins." The rabbi said, "We all hope that God forgives but how can we be sure? We can't put ourselves in the shoes of God." So he said, "Well, I was standing thinking about what I had done during the past year. It is true, I have done some things which are not okay, I was not very kind to my wife, I didn't talk to her respectfully. In my business I did a few small things which were not okay. I was not completely honest the whole year. And I have a couple of other things which I would not like to mention now. But, I asked forgiveness and had a self search about this. But, then I thought about what God had done this past year. I saw around me women who had become widows, children who lost their parents, catastrophes all over the world. And I said those things were pretty grievous sins. Now let us make a deal, I said

But the oxygen, without which the flames of hate could not sustain themselves nor spread far and wide, was the indifference of the so-called 'periphery'. The emotional neutrality of unconcerned millions, well protected from the danger of guilt, or even just undue sadness. Such is the stuff of which genocides are made...

Denial and indifference provide the milieu in which misfortunes can operate at leisure and hate can thrive, uninhibited by the large periphery of 'neutral' individuals. Their hold on the human psyche is not a weak one, and unless broken, or at least significantly weakened, active compassion remains just a noble and unattainable goal. The difficulty of that task is matched only by its importance.

Shlomo Brezntiz
Israel

to God, if you forgive me my small things, I will forgive you your big things. I am positive that God accepted this deal."

The rabbi took hold of the man's collar. He said, "You stupid fool! You had a very strong point. With this point you should have asked for forgiveness not just for yourself but for the whole Jewish people, for the whole world, the whole of humanity! Instead, you were only thinking about your own salvation."

I think this is part of the core of 'our problem', I deliberately am saying 'our problem'. As a religious leader, I think I can speak for all religious leaders. We have not done our job if we have been preoccupied with saving ourselves, our own groups, our own constituency. We have a key which could save humanity, which can still save humanity.

We have become irrelevant to many people; we have not been faithful to the basic teachings of all true religions because the basic teaching is that when God created His creation, He created everything in species and in groups. Only one piece of creation was not created in that way: the human being. There was only one human being created. Therefore, this was what was created in the image of God. Nothing else was created in God's image but the human being. There was one human being who was supposed to be father and mother to all future human beings to teach us that when somebody kills another person, he is always killing his brother, even if he belongs to a different religion, different race, or different ethnic group.

In the bible, we learn the story of the Jews going out of Egypt. From that story we learn that we should always be in solidarity with the victims of oppression, never with the pharaohs, those who create victims. This is instructional not only for us Jews, who have this as part of our history and tradition, but for all human beings. When we Jews went out of Egypt, we learned that we must love the stranger because we once were strangers in Egypt. That is what we learn from the period of torture and enslavement, not the opposite, not bitterness and hatred. Just as we have learned this from our history, I believe that all of humankind can learn it because every people has an experience of suffering somewhere in its history. If we pull in the same direction together, we might succeed in using the key we have in a way which will open doors of happiness for all human beings.

In many ways, Jewish and Irish people have a lot in common: tragedies, great persecution, famine; many, many disasters. We Jews have been through some of the worst of periods, yet always keep an optimism and a belief in the future. When the Jews went to the gas chambers during the Second World War, many of them went with the words on their lips, "I

Hate has a twin brother — indifference. Destructiveness is produced by hate, but also by indifference.

Juan Gutierrez
Spain

believe in the coming of the Messiah." Even today, despite the suffering, we still believe it. This is a belief in Judaism which has contributed to the optimism of Jews.

What does it mean to speak about the coming of the Messiah? There is a wonderful expression in the Book of Isaiah. It concerns the sign of the coming of the Messiah: the wolf will grass with the lamb; the wolf and the lamb will lie down together.

People have said to me that this is something which is difficult to believe, that it can never happen. The truth is (and I have asked the animal experts about this) that it is possible to train a wolf and a lamb to eat grass together. That is sometimes easier to do than training human beings to tolerate each other, easier than teaching them to turn their swords into plowshares, another vision of Isaiah.

There are different ways to God, different traditions, different memories. I believe this is part of God's will also, but when it comes to human conflict, we have to be able to solve our differences around the negotiating table, to fight out our disagreements in a civilised manner, not by bombing and killing each other.

If we can start training human beings to live with their differences, I believe that when the Messiah comes, together we shall welcome Him.

We must imagine another way of being in order to refuse to accept the way things are. Otherwise, cynicism and a sense of despair enters. It is a refusal to use imagination.

Richard Kearney
Republic of Ireland

Marshall Meyer

USA

We live in perilous times. The problems facing us seem overwhelming. Everything seems out of control. We talk, we involve ourselves in intellectual debates, but we do not commit ourselves to action, to addressing the terrible wrongs in our society and in our world because too many of us think there is nothing we can do as individuals. This is a spiritual problem, not just a matter of strategy.

We know there are problems in Northern Ireland. We know there are problems in former Yugoslavia. We know there are problems around the world. We know the issues. We know the source of the problems. We have the intelligence and know-how to address the problems, but we lack the courage and the political will to do something about them. What we lack is a commitment to action.

In April 1993 I participated in the "Anne Frank in the World" project at Thornhill College. I spoke to young people, Protestants and Catholics, from all over the northwest of Ireland who came to Derry to see the Anne Frank exhibition, to learn what it was all about, to study and ask questions. Invariably, they were moved, even a little shocked, by the photographs in the exhibition. When it was time for me to speak to them, they asked me, "What's the point of the exhibition? Given our world today, have we learned anything since 1945?"

These are profound questions, not easy to respond to, much less answer. We talked about Sarajevo in former Yugoslavia, a city enduring a medieval siege. Some people estimate that since the beginning of the devastating civil war in the Balkans, 120,000 people have been killed and more than 200,000 wounded. These are civilians, men, women, and children, not soldiers. Does anybody care? It is as if the United States, Canada, and the countries of Western Europe are spectators in a stadium, watching, but not participating in the action. Is it that they do not know what to do, or is it that they do not have the political will or moral determination to do it? How many more people have to die? What has to happen before we find the courage to address the issues?

On the island of Ireland, how much longer does it have to bleed before there is peace between the two main traditions, before peace becomes more than a wish, becomes an actual reality? How many more people have to be maimed or murdered before we do

President Mary Robinson spoke about the fact that we have become onlookers as opposed to participants shaping society in positive, humane ways. She was talking about what is happening on the island of Ireland, but she could just as well have been talking about what is happening in other parts of the world. We constantly see images on TV of hatred and brutality in South Africa or from around the world. The reality is that we can make a cup of coffee or a phone call while simultaneously we watch someone die in front of us on our television screen. These images will numb us, unless we find a way to deal with them.

Sheena Duncan
South Africa

something about it, before we learn to create community? Community is not some abstract utopia. Community takes work. It is made up of individuals who feel empowered to do more than talk about problems, people who are prepared to do something specific, people who are prepared to work together for the good of the whole.

Human beings are not disconnected atoms floating around in space. We have roots, identities, and faith traditions, but we constantly have to re-examine the hypotheses of our roots, our identities, our inherited faith traditions. Rabbi Abraham Joshua Heschel, my esteemed teacher, used to ask, "What constitutes being human, personhood?" We often struggled with that question, debated it. I still do. In one of his books, he addressed that question himself. "What constitutes being human, personhood" is

> The ability to be concerned for other human beings. Animals are concerned for their own instinctive needs. The degree of our being human stands in direct proportion to the degree in which we care for others… To be human we must know what humanity means, how to acquire, how to preserve it. Being human is both a fact and a demand, a condition and an expectation. Our being human is always on trial, full of risk, precarious; man is always in danger of forfeiting his humanity… Just as death is the liquidation of human being, dehumanization is the liquidation of being human (Heschel, *The Insecurity of Freedom,* 25, 26).

Rabbi Heschel, one of the great thinkers of the twentieth century, also used to ask us, "From the perspective of the bible, who is man?" It is an important question: Who is man? Heschel often reminded us that God's dream is to have humankind as a partner in the drama of creation. What does this mean? It means that by whatever we do, or fail to do, we advance or obstruct the drama of redemption. We either reduce or enhance the power of evil in our world.

How can we pray to God and not show compassion and a zeal for justice, not theoretical justice, but concrete legal and economic justice? We cannot be a partner with God in the continuing creation of this world without seeking out inequality and doing justice. We are too comfortable with the dogmas that lie in our minds, but not in our hearts. They do not motivate us enough to action on behalf of others. You cannot have a vital faith and be a complacent human being in this world.

I am interested in questions, not in answers. By the time an answer is given to an ultimate question, it no longer addresses me where I am. Such a stance does violence to people who like answers, who are uncomfortable living with questions. Many people like answers.

Many like neat dogmas. It saves us the trouble of having to work things out for ourselves. Living with questions is disturbing, but maturity is the ability to live with questions.

We must continue to ask questions, so we can revise the rigid doctrinal orthodoxies upon which the 'certainties' that divide us rest, or we shall very soon destroy our planet and ourselves.

Michael Harbottle, Juan Gutierrez, and Frauke Gutierrez

Wiktor Leyk

Poland

My roots are in two nations, Germany and Poland. I think that we people of the border have a special unique mission to build bridges beyond hate.

In Poland there are 140 political parties. Twenty-nine are represented in the parliament. Apart from a tendency towards European integration, there exists an attempt to build a religious, Catholic, national state which gives majorities the right to overrule minorities. This situation provokes flames of intolerance among Poland's national and religious minorities.

In Poland, religious matters were stifled for the forty years of 'real socialism'. The separation of church and state existed; religion was every citizen's private matter. Because of its size, the Catholic Church was a natural place for the activity of political opposition. It played a major role in the subversion of the totalitarian system. During this time, the Catholic Church's relations and partnership with other churches was ecumenical in spirit.

These days the situation has changed. Emotions are running very high. Ecumenical cooperation between the Catholic Church and the Protestant community has become quite limited. The Catholic Church still wants to have a major influence on political life, but the Church tries to impose its religious perspective on the state. This is demonstrated by compulsory religious instruction in school, the prohibition and punishment of abortion, and the control of electoral canvassing in Churches. The Catholic Church even has exclusive use of private radio and TV stations. The structure of the Catholic Church differs more and more from the democratic system that we are trying to create in Poland. This situation is causing anxiety among many citizens and has created a split in Polish society.

The problem of intolerance is a challenge in my country. Intolerance is responsible for a chauvinistic antisemitism, but it is an antisemitism without Jews. Refugees from Romania and Russia also are targets of xenophobia. There is widespread condemnation of homosexuals and drug addicts. There is discrimination against people suffering from AIDS.

The phenomenon of intolerance is caused by ignorance. The remedy for ignorance is information and education. The recognised moral and intellectual authorities must play a major role.

Our society had an egalitarian nature for forty years; education and health care were free of charge, employment and living rates were guaranteed. The current shifts in society have brought about the closure of factories and an increase in unemployment. More and more people are suffering from poverty.

The economic situation has caused many people to emigrate. It has turned politically oriented youth into radicals. In such a situation, it does not take much to stir up hatred and conflict. Can we in Poland create an open society? Can we set up democratic mechanisms and structures? Can the stabilisation of borders around a country contribute to controlling conflict inside that country? Important roles in controlling conflict must be played by social organisations. The YMCA is one of the non-government organisations in Poland which is trying to develop programmes against hatred and intolerance.

One of the reasons for the beginning of the YMCA movement in Poland years ago was to create a youth programme in opposition to nationalist, primitive beliefs. We suggested friendship, more democratic ways of thinking, tolerance for different ideas and beliefs. We believe international contacts are the best way to become acquainted with different cultures, traditions and approaches. Young people, while working and playing together, can get to know one another and learn to accept differences. It is a gradual process, but it will bring results. The YMCA wants to prove that religious, national, and cultural categories are not disadvantages but values which enrich civilisation and ourselves and make us citizens of the world.

Social life has a dynamic nature and new threats are constantly emerging. The only chance for human civilisation to avoid self destruction is the acceptance of pluralism and differences within a democratic system of values. This is a source and safeguard of development.

JOHN CASEY

Switzerland

If we look at the demographics of our world community of 5.5 billion people, we can see the potential impact of religion: 30% are Christians — predominantly in Europe and the Americas; 18% are Moslem — predominantly in the Middle East, Asia and Africa; 26% are other religions; 5% are animists (worshippers of nature); and the remaining 21% are atheists (people of no religion). Thus, 79% of the world's population are people who embrace a set of theological principles. Those theological principles often form the bedrock of their cultural identities, values, and beliefs.

Has organised religion, or even the practice of religion, contributed to a lessening of hatred or a lessening of our deepest differences, now or in the past? Because of my strong beliefs in the power of the supernatural and in the life and teachings of Jesus Christ, I wish I could answer affirmatively, but, unfortunately, I think the contrary more often has been the norm. Religion often is, sad to say, a divisive and negative force that has been used successfully to divide us rather than to unite us.

Religion has been used as the ultimate weapon in a win/lose model of community management. It has spawned hatred and exploited our deepest differences in both active and passive ways. Positive inter-faith dialogue and community building often is led by the people themselves — not the institutions of religion, education, and government. Religion is the flash point of conflict all over our world today: Armenia, Yugoslavia, Sri Lanka, Pakistan and India, Burma [or Myanmar], the Middle East, Sudan, Nigeria, and throughout Africa. It is a tension in almost every community of the world. Religion and government leaders often exploit the powerful emotional depths of people's religious convictions and values. They try to achieve their own political or narrow institutional and personal objectives at the expense of peace and justice.

Almost all hatred is based on fear and ignorance. Ignorance is the lack of a basic knowledge and understanding of that which we fear. Religion and education either can help us narrow the gap of knowledge and understanding; or, they can fuel our fears and teach us through commission or omission how to hate.

Institutions — religious, educational, and others — must be challenged to reform their image and to serve the broader, more common interests of a community. But, let us not sit and wait for that to happen. Just as community people throughout Northern Ireland are increasingly taking charge of their own moral destiny, people in leadership positions throughout the world must serve as instruments to support and assist people to take control of their own communities, of their moral and ethical destinies, and to gain understanding and skill to resolve their own conflicts which otherwise promote deep differences and fuel the fires of hatred. There are global matters and processes that must be addressed and tended to, but the larger purposes cannot be realistically achieved in the absence of grassroots community and people processes. Religion and education should be interactive processes that affirm all reality and that affirm, enlighten and teach us about our deepest differences, so that we can move beyond hate.

John Hume, Kadar Asmal, and Martin McGuinness

Fatima Nahara and Mai Thanh

Embracing The Challenges

EphREM RUTaboba

Many of us tend to be re-active rather than pro-active. That is, in situations of crisis, instead of initiating, or being pro-active, we respond to the situation. If we want to create a new future, we have to start challenging the way we think, the way we perceive and react to each other. We have to start looking at what is best in each other, at what is important.

It has always been a source of amazement to me that when you ask a Ugandan — "What kind of Uganda do you want in the future?" — most people do not have a clear picture of the kind of Uganda they want. We have been fighting for some time in Uganda. We are focused on an ailing economy, on who eventually will be in power, rather than on the kind of Uganda we want, a country that is prosperous, peaceful, secure, and strong, filled with healthy children.

Until such time as we start defining the kind of communities we want to build, the kind of world we want to have, we are only going to be talking about processes, responding in an ad hoc kind of way to situations of crisis, focusing on what is unimportant.

I have seen people move from being powerless to taking destiny into their own hands. People can do that when they have a common vision, a common purpose. That is the role of leadership: to inspire and encourage a common purpose and a common vision. If people have that they can work together, they can rise above prejudices, transcend traditional barriers, create necessary coalitions, harness resources, human and financial, and work together on what is important.

Ehud Olmert

Israel _____

People talk about the contribution of psychologists, educators, preachers, and rabbis, among others, to the question, "How can we get beyond hate and live with our deepest differences?" I want to draw attention to the importance of political leaders.

The question people everywhere are trying to find the solution to is "What kind of political mechanism can provide a reasonable solution to the conflicts and hatreds plaguing our world, our particular situation?" I think the only political mechanism that can do it is one that takes into consideration the legitimate fears of the parties involved. Instead of trying to understand the other side, each party is usually trying to justify its own prejudices and biases about the other side.

If the question is, "What can be done on the level of person to person relationships to reduce hatred?," the contribution of the 'helping professions' is relevant, but if the question is, "What can be done to change the circumstances that encourage people to give in to temptation to express hatred towards others?" the power to effect that change lies with political leaders. While they cannot automatically reduce hatred, they can use their political power to reduce the temptation of people to express hatred towards each other. Political leaders can help to change the psychological climate which affects the quality of relationships among people.

Think for a moment about former American President Jimmy Carter: his most important achievement as President of the United States was his participation in the efforts to bring about peace between Israel and Egypt. To this day, I think he is still fascinated by the meeting between President Anwar Sadat and Prime Minister Menachem Begin. It is a perfect example of what politicians can do at a particular juncture in the history of their own people. Political decisions will not reduce hate, but they may reduce the circumstances within which hate can be expressed and that is more than just a little important.

How are fears born? They are born because of differences in tradition and history; they are born because of differences in emotional, political, and national circumstances. Because of such differences, people fear they cannot live together. If we are to overcome such fear, a credible, healthy political process must be carefully and patiently developed, a political

Free societies are no protection against hatred. We all know that Adolf Hitler and Nazi Germany evolved from the results of a free election. We do not like to remember that the Founding Fathers of our democratic government in America approved human slavery, and for almost two centuries, our country condoned and legalized racial discrimination... These are just cautionary words to guard us against an over-reliance on democracy as a certain deterrence to conflict.

Jimmy Carter
USA

84

process that does not aim to change the other or to overcome differences, but that allows each side to live peacefully in spite of the differences.

James Mehaffey and Terry Waite

Ruben Zamora

El Salvador

The deepest differences are those which destroy the rationale for being human and, therefore, destroy the rationale for going beyond hate. We cannot go 'beyond hate' and live with such differences. I am referring to 'differences' that are so deep they destroy the nature of human beings. We see, for example, what is happening to the children of Somalia and Rwanda. What is going on there? Human beings are being destroyed and that destruction is based on differences with which we cannot live. These differences can be avoided if we work to avoid or to change them.

I can live with some 'differences'. Indeed, we can sing a hymn to those differences from which the very richness of all human beings develop. But there are differences which deprive the human being of his/her own nature; those we cannot accept. We must overcome them if one day we are to overcome hate.

It is important to distinguish between the source of hate and the 'catalyser' for hate. Only when these two elements are present can we talk about hate as a social phenomenon.

The source of hate is always deprivation of some kind. Material deprivation — poverty — or spiritual deprivation — lack of liberty or liberties — these are the sources of hate. But, of themselves they are not enough for hate as a social phenomenon, unless there is the other element: the catalyser. These are symbols which freeze deprivation into rigid systems of belief, such as tribal superiority, religious bigotry, racism, and a narrow concept of nationalism or culture. In any society, there may be deprivation. That deprivation may produce anger. And it is possible that this does not produce hate because there is no catalyser to fix the deprivation and transpose it into religious difference, cultural difference, national difference, or ethnic difference.

In South Africa and in Northern Ireland, one source of hate is deprivation. Differences, economic and social, exist. In both countries, there is hatred because there also is the additional element which has frozen the deprivation in another context. In South Africa, it is colour; in Northern Ireland it is religion. Hate is different from social anger in the sense that hate is social anger that has been fixed or frozen.

Many conflicts have a common element. About one hundred and fifty years ago, William Cobbett wrote, "I defy you to agitate a fellow with a full stomach." While I think that is a bit too simple an approach to the question of poverty, I would underline the fact that questions related to the situation of housing, employment, and social inequalities must be addressed if one wants to discover how tensions between different groups in the population are to be reduced.

**Pieter Dankert
Netherlands**

Our problem in El Salvador is not a problem of hate. In my country, in the last twelve years, more than eighty thousand people have been assassinated for political reasons. My country has the distinction of being one of the worst in terms of cruelty, killing, and torturing people.

Yet, in El Salvador we signed a peace agreement in 1992 and — surprisingly — since then nobody has been killed by the two warring factions. Other people have been killed for reasons that have to do with common crimes, or occasionally because of some political incident, but there are no more incidents between the two armies. The United Nations now say that El Salvador is one of the few examples in which a cease-fire has been successful.

If we have been successful at this moment in El Salvador, we must look to the future and discern how we can avoid hate. What in El Salvador might be a source of new anger that could be converted into hate?

The first possibility is that the expectations of people will not be fulfilled. Such unfulfilled expectations could become a source of anger among our people. The second is the incapacity of our society to recognise that potential sources of anger still exist and that a negotiating process will not solve all problems. Negotiations allow a society to transform itself from a militarised into a demilitarised society. But negotiations alone will not allow us to move from being one of the most polarised societies in Latin America into a less polarised society. If we do not address these issues in the next two years, that anger could boil over into violence.

One of the reasons our country could revert to anger is the passivity of civil society. During the last five years, the possibility for negotiations started with civil society in El Salvador. By civil society, I mean church organisations, trade unions, non-governmental organisations (NGO's), — essential components of society. They were the ones who legitimised the negotiating process. Yet, once the negotiations started, it seemed that civil society started to lose ground because the two warring parties, the government and the guerrillas, and the United Nations took over. They started to discuss behind locked doors, and the civil society started to become more passive towards the whole process. This is the danger now, that civil society will lose the initiative it had earlier.

Another potential source of anger is the 'formal' rather than the 'real' fulfilment of the agreement. By this, I mean saying that we are fulfilling the agreement, when in fact we are not changing society. We need to work at changing the daily reality for many people.

I believe we are making a fundamental mistake if we equate resistance against abuses of power, or against states who use force to subjugate and denigrate people with hate. Unquestionably some people may hate others through ignorance. Some good people may even hate, but I believe it is a mistake to think that the overwhelming body of people who are involved in any struggle we care to examine, be it passive political action or armed challenge, hate.

Caoimighin O'Caolain
Republic of Ireland

It is important to develop a strategy to avoid anger that could be converted into hate. There are three fundamental ways to try to do it, and they have to be worked at simultaneously.

First, we have to overcome basic deprivation in society. If we can not do that, it does not matter how many meetings of reconciliation we have, or how wonderful the initiatives we take in terms of reconciling rich and poor. In the end, poverty and deprivation are going to generate anger, no matter what we say. Second, we must develop a strategy for channelling anger. The process must be one in which all people feel involved. And third, we must find ways to avoid the fixing power of the catalyser within religion, education, and culture. We need religion, education, race, and colour to bring people together, not to separate them as has happened in the past. We must ensure that they do not become frozen in identity with either the dominant or the deprived. If they do, anger will turn to hate, and we shall not be able to move beyond hate and learn to live with healthy differences.

The openness and democratic character of the ANC in South Africa and the ideological flexibility of the forces of the left in El Salvador were key factors in the avoidance of fixing social anger into hate.

But if you have the development of a high level of ideological rigidity, as with the Shining Path in Peru, it is quite possible that social anger will become fixed into hate. Without other symbols to transform a struggle between a vast impoverished majority, suffering incredible injustice because of the global economic situation, and their national elites, it is possible to fix ideological rigidity into a level of brutality and hatred which is just as damaging as the fixation produced by different forms of religious, ethnic, and national fundamentalisms.

Ian Linden
Great Britain

Mark Durkan and Ruben Zamora

88

Maria Diokno

I come from the Philippines, a poor country colonised virtually its entire life. We were colonised for four hundred years by Spain, then by the Americans, and during World War II, we were occupied for three years by Japan. And under Ferdinand Marcos, we had fourteen years of dictatorship.

In my country, we have deep social problems. There is a tremendous disparity between rich and poor. We face an armed conflict, largely between the government and a Marxist revolutionary group led by the National Democratic Front. There are other armed parties as well. One is a Muslim group; another is a faction of the armed forces which not long ago tried forcibly to remove the President, at that time Cory Aquino, from power.

Before we can get beyond hate, we must look at the causes of hate. The situation in my country cannot be viewed simply from an individual perspective, however. We are not talking about a quarrel between lovers or friends, but about a conflict between peoples. The causes of this conflict and of the hatred which fuels it are political. Therefore, the solution must be political. Before we can figure out how to correct the situation, we first have to understand why the situation exists. To do so, we must go beyond the psychological explanation of hate — in itself, a very complex emotion — and critique the structures of society that have spawned inequality and injustice and, in turn, nurtured anger, hatred, and conflict.

In the Philippines, education, a seemingly non-political aspect of national life, was used to turn us into submissive people. We were taught that Philippinos were lazy, that the best way to progress was to become 'little brown Americans', which is what we were called for a long time. To this day, there are Philippinos who are confused about their identity. We constantly were told there was nothing of value in our own culture. Such education does not help people change the structures of society. Such education is not liberating, but enslaving.

Ferdinand Marcos often told the Philippine people, "You have to make a choice. Do you want to develop into a rich country, or do you want to be free? If you want to develop into a rich country, you had better accept my style of government." He used the poverty of the people as a weapon against the people. Since Marcos' time, we have heard others apply the same kind of thinking to other situations. It is always the same: You must make a choice.

Maria Diokno

Currently, there is a debate going on in the human rights community. It concerns the issue of whether or not those who have committed crimes, particularly tortures and those responsible for making people 'disappear', should be forgiven. Sometimes the timidity of my people is mistaken for forgiveness of the very people who committed these crimes. In fact, it is not forgiveness, but a sense of powerlessness that people feel. The relatives of the victims feel powerless. They can not go to court because if they do, they are not certain that when they return home they will be safe.

My people often are criticised for being timid, but when we show our anger or displeasure, people are shocked and say things like, "But you are Asians. You should not be feeling that way." Well, my people are angry, and we have been angry for a very long time.

If you look at our history, or the histories of many other oppressed countries in the world, you will see that history is actually a long struggle of liberation and justice. For a number of years, some of us from different churches — Catholic and Protestant — and from different sectors of society — farmers, trade unionists, professionals, women, students, 'Peace Advocates' — have been coming together, trying to pressure the Government and the National Democratic Front to meet and dialogue.

It is not easy to get two parties who have been in constant conflict over a long period of time to sit across the table and be civil toward one another. It is even more difficult when you are concerned with the interconnectedness of issues, as we are. We try not to fall into the trap of some people, especially people in government, who want to isolate and simplify issues. Our vision of peace is not simply the absence of physical violence. It is far more complex. It is peace based on justice.

When the government brought in paramilitary forces in order to defeat the rebel forces, they said that those of us who opposed the use of paramilitary forces — I am one of them — sided with the communists. I once said to some members of the military, "Gentlemen, after fighting for fourteen years to defeat dictatorship and restore democracy, are you telling me that if I oppose the use of paramilitary forces I am a communist? Are you trying to tell me that I cannot be me? I do not accept such an idea."

One of the central questions we face in our deeply polarised society is how to live with our deep differences. I believe we can live with our differences only when there is justice. And what is justice? Justice is a preferential option for the poor. It is a concrete option for the poor, the powerless, the under-privileged. It is a concept of justice that goes beyond mere political democracy. It is biased. It is not neutral. For us in the Third World, justice is also the

Gaining a voice is a common metaphor among women for a sense of empowerment. But having a sense of voice does not always result in feeling heard, feeling you have a right to speak, having one's words register with others. Who gets heard is almost always a matter of social power and

capacity to decide for ourselves how we want to live and how we want to develop.

In our work for justice and peace, we take into consideration the policies of international creditor institutions whose rigid policies and repayment schedules have helped to devastate local economies, heaping greater misery on the poor. The economic disparities we experience in our part of the world are increasingly felt in the richer parts of the world. We need to be cognizant of the connectedness of economic policies — often made in one part of the world — and human well-being affected in another part of the world.

Many of us are engaged in community organising — formally and informally — from concrete programmes of action designed to empower communities to programmes of conscientisation [education to raise consciousness]. We all know that ordinary citizens want a just resolution of conflict. What is it that spells the difference between success and failure? The active participation and involvement of ordinary citizens. Popular organisations can mount pressure on governments, even on parties in conflict, to listen to the needs of the people. Individually we can do very little, but together we can do a great deal.

People around the world, in poor countries and in rich ones, are organising. All over the world people are engaging in the struggle against power structures that exclude. People are pushing for change. Let us not obstruct their actions. Rather, let us join them in their struggle for justice.

the dynamics of subordination and dominance. In many cultures and subcultures, silence is associated with gender (men talk, women listen). Focusing in on a person's experience of silence can help one learn a great deal about how any disempowered person deals with silence and ultimately confronts and challenges the dominant voices of his or her culture.

Finding their voice as women should be foremost on women's personal and political agenda. How can we share what we know, see and value if we do not speak? How can we confront hatred or difference if we do not speak? Do we stand silent in agony when we hear about rapes in Bosnia, about women prostituted in Sudan, about children dying in Somalia, about violence in the lives in those closest to us? To quote an Afro-American poet,

"We can sit in our corners mute forever while our sisters and ourselves are wasted, while our children are distorted and destroyed, while our earth is poisoned; we can sit in our safe corners mute as bottles, and we will be no less afraid… While we wait in silence for that final luxury of fearlessness, the weight of that silence will choke us." (Lorde, *Sister Outsider*).

Nancy Goldberger
USA

INEZ McCORMACK

Northern Ireland _____

Some months ago I chaired a conference on community economic development. Seated on the platform were senior public servants, the people who run Northern Ireland. They were talking about their economic policies and how they develop them. Seated on the floor listening to them were community development activists and community representatives, quite a few of them from dispossessed areas. From the platform came comfortable explanations about what had gone wrong, about how things were going to get better. From the floor came screams of outrage. The people on the floor were screaming, but the people on the platform were not listening.

One of the things I am interested in is power: Who has it? Who does not? How is it exercised? Who legitimizes it? When power is exercised as dominance that excludes people, the structures of society supporting such an exercise of power inevitably produce inequalities and injustice and must be challenged. Sometimes there is no capacity for change within the individuals who control those structures because they think their exercise of power is a reasonable norm of how society should be organised. If that is the case, I think we need to broaden our view of hatred. Power exercised as dominance that excludes people is hatred. It may be hatred exercised in a very civilized, gentle form, but it is hatred nevertheless, a hatred that inflicts damage and destroys human beings economically, socially, and politically.

What was missing at that conference was an agenda of equality of a different kind of power. Not that those who held power should admit their mistakes in order to be vilified, but they should have been prepared to hear what was being said, prepared to accept the fact that they had exercised their responsibility poorly. They should have begun to recognize that it was time to exercise power responsibly by a process of involving those whose lives are affected by their decision making.

Between those on the floor and those on the platform there was no dialogue. The people on the platform were defending the status quo, and the people on the floor were raging but no-one was listening. In actual fact, the people on the floor were looking for a voice so that they could be heard.

One of the problems we have about getting to the truth in Northern Ireland is that statistics tell you one thing, for example, they may tell you that power, jobs, houses are with the Protestants. But when you work with Protestants who have also lived in poverty, such truth will be rejected, because it is neither their reality nor their truth.

Mari Fitzduff
Northern Ireland

Primo Levi is an Italian writer who before his death wrote about his experiences during the Holocaust. I find his writings difficult to read. He wrote out of a sense of his duty to bear witness for those victims of hate whose voices have been stilled. A guard in one of the Nazi death camps once told him that "in the unlikely event that you survive, it does not matter, because nobody will listen to what you have to say."

When people who have not been listened to in the past embrace their worth and assert it in society, existing power structures are called into question. They are called 'troublemakers'. What the people on the platform viewed as unreasonable contributions from the floor were in fact contributions that did not fit in with their view of how things should be run. In effect, they said, "We've never involved you before. We are going to involve you now, but we are going to involve you on our terms." Such a situation does not create dialogue.

How do you create dialogue with those who hold power when, in effect, you are told that dialogue will be on the terms of those who hold power? I, personally, am not interested in dialogue on those terms. I am interested in dialogue between equals.

What is it that enables the powerless to become equal? Can the equation only be achieved by the gun? We say it can not be the gun. The people who hold power say it can not be achieved by the gun. What then can it be? What are the mechanisms that help to create a dialogue between equals? What we know is that to have dialogue everyone must have the right to be heard and to have a say. If we cannot provide those alternative mechanisms and show that they produce results, then those who take the route of violence will, quite rightly, consider that our stance supports the status quo, that we are supporting their oppression while easing our pacifist consciences.

I live in a society where such mechanisms do not exist for the people I represent. The people I represent are not the 'interesting' people of history. They are not the people with guns. The people I represent are home helps, school cleaners, and others. Mostly, they are women, the poor, people who have not made themselves 'interesting'. They are called 'troublemakers'. Well, my message is that they will go on making trouble because that trouble is about the right to be heard in dignity; to be listened to with respect and to have some say in the decisions which affect their lives. What are the mechanisms which will ensure that?

Most of my working life has been about enabling people who have no sense of their own voice to constructively channel their anger. Recently some of the women members of our union produced a book. These women are school cleaners, school meal workers, hospital

Women have much to say about the topic of difference in our world, because women have been thought of as 'the other' since time began. The history of 'humankind' has been written by men. Science, philosophy, and most of our social and religious institutions are the products of men. Man is the centrepiece and yardstick against which all is measured. Women have been considered at various points in history as imperfect or deficient men, or as not-man, that is, as 'the other'. Women have been feared and revered. Women have become, in almost all cultures across history, mythic in their otherness. Woman has been the symbol of mystery, raw nature, life; woman also has been the symbol of evil and danger. Women have been depicted as temptresses who lure rational men to their downfall, if not their death. Not only have women been 'the other' — strange and different — women have been the shadow... In most societies, women, like children, get the message that they are to be seen and not heard. I believe that women, from their historical marginalised position as 'the other in the shadow', have much to say about learning to live with difference. That is, if we can overcome our silence, find our voice, and speak.

Nancy Goldberger
USA

93

domestics, home care workers. They are among the invisible women in society. In their book they recounted the history of their mothers and grandmothers. They told how their mothers and grandmothers died in childbirth, how they died in the fields, how they were people who kept the world running but were marginalised, not consulted in the decision-making processes of the world. In that history, they spelled out their own reality. These women wrote their book, not to be victims, but to ensure that unlike their mothers and grandmothers, they will have a voice in the decisions which affect their lives.

Young people discussing conference themes in small groups.

EUGENE WEINER

Israel

During the twenty-five years I haved lived in Israel, I have come to see that the Arabs have some very good reasons to hate Jews, and Jews have some very good reasons to hate Arabs. There are extremists on both sides. They are often quite eloquent about their interests, and they can convincingly document reasons why one side or the other should continue to hate the other. And yet, in Israel we Jews and Arabs have no other alternative than coexistence.

Coexistence is the minimal, least demanding way for people to relate to one another positively. It is not the same thing as love. It may not even be the same thing as friendship. To the contrary, it is an expression of distance, and an acknowledgement that boundaries will remain, that the possibilities of misunderstanding will never completely disappear. It is informed by an attitude of 'live and let live', and that is precisely the message.

Coexistence is an ideal without illusions. Its objective is not the seamless union of opposites, but a practical relationship of mutual respect among opposites. Coexistence does not deny distinctiveness; it disarms it, and robs it of its power to wound or kill. It does not fear separation; it seeks to organize separation rationally and compassionately. In a pluralistic society, ethnic and cultural differences are not abolished. They are legitimated, and society strives to guarantee that the law will be blind to them.

Moving beyond hate and learning to live with differences is about managing to get through the day without dominating others in a way that dehumanizes them and that enables you to continue on with your life. This is an enormous achievement. It may not be a solution, but then, I generally am apprehensive about solutions. I am happy if people who hate each other — and who even have good reasons for hating each other — can make it together without engaging in great violence. What getting beyond hate and learning how to live with differences is about is coexistence, a practical relationship of mutual respect among opposites. It is not easy to achieve, but when you have no alternative, it is worth trying to achieve.

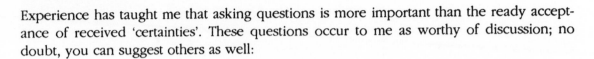

Paddy Doherty

Northern Ireland

Experience has taught me that asking questions is more important than the ready acceptance of received 'certainties'. These questions occur to me as worthy of discussion; no doubt, you can suggest others as well:

- What is not 'beyond' hate, but 'before' hate?

- How can a city like Derry, which has experienced twenty-five years of conflict and growth, use its experience to help other communities around the world learn to live with their differences?

- How do organisations outside the ordinary political structures of society create space for 'reluctant', civil, religious, and political leaders to negotiate with each other?

- How can we network with and use the experiences of other communities around the world who have resolved their difficulties of living together to challenge our own efforts?

- How do we train 'log jam' breakers?

- What skills do we need to develop to ensure that the extraordinary achievements of ordinary people who live together despite their differences are projected and communicated as effectively as the forces which divide and diminish humanity?

- What kind of political mechanisms must we develop to provide reasonable solutions to the conflicts and hatreds plaguing our particular situation, our world?

- What evidence of hope is there that human beings can work together despite their differences to achieve what they want?

- What steps can I take to move 'beyond hate'?

- Which shall I choose: to stay with the 'certainties' of the past, or to risk the 'uncertainties' of the future?

- How can I 'remember' for the future?

Paddy Doherty

Hate is human, but human development must find a way to overcome it.

Juan Gutierrez
Spain

96

JOHN HUME

Northern Ireland _____

Getting 'beyond hate' is a journey. We must remember that people are at various places on this journey. Some have begun the journey. They give heart to those who have not yet embarked on it. Others are more cautious; they are hesitant about beginning the journey. We must remember, however, that we are all involved in the process of learning. We are all students when it comes to moving beyond hate, and we must be wary of accusing, lecturing, or ignoring those we perceive to be at a different place in the journey than we are.

In every situation of hatred, the complexity and corrosion of truth confronts each of us. Each side has its own 'truth', a truth it uses to define or rationalize events in such a way as to affirm its own sense of victimization, to justify its response. Just as our past history contributes to our present prejudices, so, too, do our present prejudices contribute to paralysing our future. We all should question history, because history values violence and war. It does not usually find peaceful change interesting. Such history makes a normative contribution to violence and to expressions of hatred.

Challenges to our traditional concept of history, and they are heavy challenges if we think about them, are important elements in the task of moving beyond hate, especially in deeply divided societies where history — our respect for the past — tends to dominate our present and paralyse our future. These challenges emphasize a consciousness of humanity, rather than the insensitivity or elitism operative in most traditional histories. If we all applied these challenges to our particular situation, it could undermine the myths and crude stereotypes, both of ourselves and of others, which are the shorthand of so much traditional history which becomes the graffiti of current hatred.

Acknowledging past wrongs and repenting are essential first steps toward reconciliation. After periods of hurt or violence, we can only reconcile with others who want to reconcile, but first we must admit our wrongs and determine to do better. Such repentance is a vital means by which we give each other confidence that we truly want to reconcile, that we want to release ourselves from the disabilities of prejudice, false justification and guilt, and that we hope to release others from the disabling effects of the hurt or grievance from which they suffer.

John Hume

Getting beyond hate is only part, albeit a major part, of the challenge we face in Northern Ireland. We also must learn to live with differences. In doing so, we cannot seek structures or solutions made in the image of only one particular tradition, identity, or factional outlook. We need to develop frameworks, structures, and processes which can provide for convergence of legitimacy, allegiance, and purpose. We must create means whereby we can respect and give expression to our deep differences, yet pay full and active attention to our far-reaching common interests.

While we might usefully reappraise our own respective identity to make it more inclusive, less exclusive, we must take care not to try to assume the identity of others or try to rewrite another's definition of his/her own identity. A difficult part of recognizing individual 'truth' is to allow others to define their own identities, then seek to accommodate those identities with one's own.

In the past two decades in Northern Ireland, more than three thousand people have lost their lives. In this small part of the world, that is one out of every five hundred people. It is the equivalent of one hundred thousand people in Britain. Not only have lives been lost and people maimed, but in Belfast, which has the highest level of church attendance in Western Europe, it has been necessary to build not one, but thirteen walls to separate and protect one group of Christians from another. Those walls are a lesson for everyone involved in conflict anywhere in the world, because they are the result of pushing difference to the point of division, and they are an indictment of everybody involved in our problem, whether they be Unionists, Nationalists, or the British. Those walls are a major challenge to all of us because of what they mean. Our attitudes, past and present, have built them, and if we are ever to bring them down, we must be prepared to re-examine those attitudes. If we can meet that challenge, we will make a major contribution to areas of conflict everywhere.

It is important to distinguish between the need to cherish 'difference' and the desirability of including others in the decision-making. When we look at the two major traditions in our society, we can see that both have some rethinking to do so that each can become more inclusive. To insist on holding all power in their own hands, as the Unionists have done until now, betrays a 'siege mentality' based on fear, a fear that at some point there may be revenge from those whom they have excluded. As human beings, we have a duty to remove completely from our society the notion of revenge so that we can develop an atmosphere in which people have the freedom to change.

We Nationalists also have some rethinking to do. We are heirs of a tradition that has been handed down to us that says territory is more important than people. Our piece of earth

Many times one is in a situation of helplessness and unable to assess what is 'the truth'. It is important to make a distinction between truth as a fact, or a cluster of facts, and the search for truth. The difference usually is not between 'the truth' and a lie, but between partial truth and partial truth.

Juan Gutierrez
Spain

already is united; it is our people that are divided. Such a territorial approach has not made a major contribution to the healing process.

The essence of unity is the acceptance of diversity, not uniformity. It may sound like a contradiction, but every society in the world that is united is united because it accepts diversity. In Europe, the driving forces of nationalism were born largely in the nineteenth century. History will not have many kind things to say about nineteenth century nationalism, because, among other things, it created imperialism, from which the world has suffered enormously. In the twentieth century alone, the people of Europe have slaughtered each other by the millions twice. And yet, I am hopeful, because, despite it all, Europe is united. Where once there was animosity between deadly enemies — France and Germany, for example — today there is respect for difference. This should give hope to us all.

This fact of history imposes a duty on everyone involved in an area of conflict, a duty to study how it happened and to apply that learning. The unity of Europe represents a powerful message for all people.

The peoples of Europe learned that difference is normal, that difference is not, and should not be, a threat. Difference is enriching. It seems a simple, entirely self-evident insight, yet it is quite profound. It is a great irony to hear people in different areas of conflict bringing God or Allah down on the side of one or the other. Such people do not seem to realize that difference is the essence of creation and, in the name of God who created it, should never be a source of hatred,

Humanity transcends nationality. We are human beings before we are anything else, and it is an accident of birth where and what we were born. Therefore, it should never be a source of hatred or conflict call on God or Allah to side with them. What the Europeans decided was that difference should be accommodated and respected, that each identity should be respected, and that the way to do that was to build institutions which accommodated all identities and allowed them to work on their common interests together. By working together on their common interests, Europeans broke down prejudices and grew together. As a result, the evolution of the European Union continues.

We must find a way to apply that kind of thinking to every area of conflict. We must find a way to allow people to define their own identity. Our task is not to wipe one another out, but to discover how we can accommodate each other's differences while still preserving our own identity.

If a government has nothing to gain from stopping a war, why should they do so? People in power who have nothing to gain from peace will continue fighting for as long as they can.

Ivana Balen
Belgrade

Martin Luther King often said that our choice is simple: either we choose chaos, or we choose cohabitation. It all depends on the method one chooses. For the good of all, we must choose cohabitation. It is the only way to resolve difference. Spilling sweat is a much more important contribution to humanity than spilling blood.

One of the purposes of communication is to provide insight. If I come to an adversary with my version of the truth, as if it were definitive and infallible truth, the end result often is that no insight is gained and conflict is deepened. But if we listen to each other's stories, to one another's experiences, we begin to achieve insight. And when insight is achieved, I think we begin to get a clearer understanding of the truth of another person's story. Whenever that starts to happen, we move into situations where reconciliation becomes possible.

John Dunlop
Northern Ireland

Nelson Mandela

Nelson Mandela

Today we confer glory and hope on newborn liberty. Out of the experience of an extraordinary human disaster that lasted too long must be born a society of which all humanity will be proud. Our daily deeds as ordinary South Africans must produce an actual South African reality that will reinforce humanity's belief in justice, strengthen its confidence in the nobility of the human soul, and sustain our hopes of a glorious life for all...

The time for healing wounds has come.
The moment to bridge the chasms that divide us has come.
The time to build is upon us.

We have, at last, achieved our political emancipation. We pledge ourselves to liberate all our people from the continuing bondage of poverty, deprivation, suffering, gender, and other discrimination.

We understand that there is no easy road to freedom. We know well that none of us acting alone can achieve success. We must, therefore, act together as a united people for national reconciliation, for nation building, for the birth of a new world.

Let there be justice for all.
Let there be peace for all.
Let there be work, bread, water and salt for all.

Let everyone know that for each person, the body, the mind, and the soul have been freed to fulfill themselves.

Inaugural Address
South Africa
1994

CONTRIBUTORS

Terry Anderson was Chief Middle East correspondent for the Associated Press and head of its Beirut bureau. Kidnapped by radical Shiite Muslims, he was held hostage for 2,454 days.

Kadar Asmal is Minister for Waters and Forestry in President Nelson Mandela's Cabinet. Mr. Asmal is also a member of the National Executive of the African National Congress (ANC). Before returning to South Africa in 1992, he lectured in Law at Trinity College, Dublin.

Ivana Balen lives in Belgrade, where she is a member of the feminist anti-war group, *Women in Black.*

Kjell Magne Bondevik is a member of the Norwegian Parliament. As Minister of Foreign Affairs (in 1990), Mr. Bondevik helped to make possible *The Anatomy of Hate* conference in Oslo.

Shlomo Breznitz is Lady Davis Professor of Psychology at the University of Haifa, Israel. He has been involved in the Beyond Hate project since its inception.

Gro Harlem Bruntland is the Prime Minister of Norway.

Jimmy Carter is a former President of the USA (1977-1981) who is active in human rights issues around the world.

John Casey is Secretary General of the World Alliance of YMCAs, the first North American to hold the post in forty years.

Lilia Cherkasskaya is Chief Expert at The Institute for Problems of Humanism and Misericordia, Moscow.

Edward Daly is the recently retired Roman Catholic Bishop of the Diocese of Derry. Bishop Daly has been active in efforts to promote peace and reconciliation between Catholics and Protestants in Northern Ireland.

Pieter Dankert is the former State Secretary for Foreign Affairs in the Netherlands. He has been actively involved in the European Parliament.

Seamus Deane is a poet, critic, and Programme Leader of the University of Notre Dame's new Irish Studies course. He is a Director of Field Day and the General Editor of *The Field Day Anthology of Irish Writing.*

Maria Diokno is Associate Dean of the College of Social Sciences and Philosophy at the University of the Philippines. She has been a member of the Government Negotiating Panel for Peace Talks with the National Democratic Front in the Philippines.

Paddy Doherty is Chief Executive of the Inner City Trust in Derry. He has extensive experience as a builder, civil rights activist, and social entrepreneur.

Sheena Duncan is Senior Vice President of the South African Council of Churches. Mrs. Duncan is also a member of the Black Sash National Executive and has long been active in human rights issues in South Africa.

John Dunlop is a former Moderator of the Presbyterian Church in Ireland.

Leo Eitinger is Professor Emeritus of Psychiatry at the University of Oslo, Norway.

Mari Fitzduff is the Director of the Northern Ireland Community Relations Council.

William J. Flynn is Chairman of the Board, Mutual of America, New York, NY, USA.

Claire Gaudiani is President of Connecticut College in New London, Connecticut, USA.

Nancy Goldberger is Professor of Psychology at The Fielding Institute, Santa Barbara, California. She is co-author of *Women's Ways of Knowing* (New York: Basic Books).

Juan Gutierrez is Coordinator of the Guernika Peace Research Centre and an acknowledged expert in conflict resolution.

John Hume is Leader of the Social Democratic and Labour Party. Mr. Hume is a member of both the British and the European Parliaments.

Lawrence Jenco is a Roman Catholic priest and a member of the Servites. Father Jenco was serving in Lebanon when he was kidnapped and held hostage by extremist Shiites for nearly two years.

Shulamith Katznelson is the Founder and Director of Ulpan Akiva in Israel.

Richard Kearney is Professor of Philosophy at University College, Dublin and Visiting European Professor at Boston College in the USA.

Brian Keenan is a Lecturer at Trinity College, Dublin. He spent almost five years as a hostage of Shiite Muslim extremists in Beirut. Mr. Keenan was born in Belfast.

Wiktor Leyk is General Director of the YMCA in Poland. He also is the founder and editor-in-chief of *Ecumenical Studies* and *Documents Quarterly* in Poland.

Ian Linden is General Secretary of the Catholic Institute for International Relations in London.

Mairead Corrigan Maguire is a co-founder of the Community of Peace People and the Committee for the Administration of Justice in Northern Ireland. Mrs. Maguire shared the 1976 Nobel Peace Prize with Betty Williams.

Nelson Mandela is President of the Republic of South Africa, having been inaugurated in 1994. He was in prison for nearly three decades during the period of apartheid. Mr. Mandela and former President F.W. DeKlerk shared the 1993 Nobel Peace Prize.

Inez McCormack is Regional Organiser for the National Union of Public Employees and a member of the Executive Committee of the Irish Congress of Trade Unions, (ICTU).

James Mehaffey is the Church of Ireland Bishop for the Diocese of Derry and Raphoe. Bishop Mehaffey is active in efforts to promote peace and reconciliation between Catholics and Protestants in Northern Ireland.

Baljeet Mehra is a psychoanalyst in private practice in London.

Michael Melchior is the Chief Rabbi of the Jewish Community in Norway. He is actively involved in humanitarian projects in Europe and Israel, where he lives with his family when he is not in Oslo.

Marshall Meyer was Senior Rabbi of Congregation B'nai Jeshurun in New York. Rabbi Meyer served for many years as the Chief Rabbi in Buenos Aires. He was active in human rights issues, prior to his sudden death in December 1993.

Bill Moyers is an American journalist and independent television producer.

Sondra Myers is Special Assistant to the Chairman of the National Endowment for the Humanities, Washingtom D.C., USA.

Mwalimu Musheshe is Administrator of the Uganda Food and Peace Project.

Richard Needham is Minister of Trade and Exports in Prime Minister John Major's Conservative government. Mr. Needham was the Under Secretary of State for Northern Ireland (1985-1992).

Caoimighin O'Caolain is a member of Sinn Fein's *Ard Combairle* (National Executive).

Garrett O'Connor is an Associate Clinical Professor of Psychiatry at the University of California, Los Angeles, USA.

Ehud Olmert is Mayor of Jerusalem, Israel.

Radim Palous is Rector of Charles University in Prague, and one of the original signatories of *Charter 77*.

Mary Robinson is President of the Republic of Ireland.

John K. Roth is Pitzer Professor of Philosophy at Claremont McKenna College in California. He is the author of many books and essays and has been involved in the Beyond Hate project from the beginning.

Ephrem Rutaboba is a civil engineer in Uganda who has been active in community development work at both the local and national levels.

Wole Soyinka was awarded the 1986 Nobel Prize in Literature, the first Nigerian to be so honoured.

David Kwang-sun Suh is a Presbyterian minister and the Dean of Ewha Women's University in Seoul, Korea. He is an active member of the World Council of Churches and a human rights activist in Korea.

Romila Thapar is a university professor in India and a scholar who has written about issues related to ethnic conflict and minorities in society.

Desmond Tutu is the Anglican Archbishop of Cape Town, South Africa. Archbishop Tutu was awarded the 1984 Nobel Peace Prize.

Terry Waite is a retired member of the staff of Lambeth Palace. Taken hostage by radical Shiite Muslims in Beirut while negotiating the release of other hostages, Mr. Waite was himself taken hostage and held for several years, being released finally in 1991.

Derick Wilson is Director of the charitable project, *Understanding Conflict and Finding Ways Out of It,* which is linked with universities in both parts of Ireland. He is also active in youth and community work in Northern Ireland.

Elie Wiesel is a distinguished author and teacher who is Andrew Mellon Professor in the Humanities at Boston University in the USA. He is the 1986 Nobel Peace Laureate. Mr. Wiesel started the 'hate project' in 1988.

Bryn Wolfe is the Quaker Representative in Sri Lanka. He is responsible for a wide range of humanitarian programmes.

Ruben Zamora is Vice President of the National Assembly in El Salvador. Mr. Zamora was a Presidential candidate in the 1994 Salvadoran elections.

Editors

Eamonn Deane is Director of Holywell Trust in Derry. He has been involved in community work for many years and is a member of many organisations concerned with social innovation. He is editor of *Fingerpost,* a monthly magazine.

Carol Rittner is an American Sister of Mercy who also is the 1994-1995 Ida E King Distinguished Visiting Scholar in Holocaust Studies at The Richard Stockton College in New Jersey, USA. Dr. Rittner is the editor of five books, most recently (with John K. Roth) of *Different Voices: Women and the Holocaust* (New York: Paragon House). She was the Director of the 1992 conference, *Beyond Hate: Living With Our Deepest Differences.*

Further Reading

- Anderson, Terry.
  ### DEN OF LIONS!
  Memoirs of Seven Years in Captivity
  New York: Hodder, 1994.

- Bergos-Debray, Elizabeth.
  ### I, RIGOBERTA MENCHU
  Story of an Indian Woman in Guatemala
  London: Verso,1984.

- Cardenal, Ernesto.
  ### NICARAGUAN NEW TIMES.
  London: Journeyman Press Ltd., 1988.

- Cataldi, Anna.
  ### LETTERS FROM SARAJEVO:
  Voices of a Beseiged City.
  London: Element Books, 1994.

- Chikane, Frank.
  ### NO LIFE OF MY OWN.
  London: Catholic Institute for International Relations, 1988.

- Dizdarevic, Zlatko.
  ### SARAJEVO: A WAR JOURNAL
  New York: Fromm International,1994.

- Frank, Anne.
  ### THE DIARY OF A YOUNG GIRL.
  New York: Washington Square Press, 1970.

- Frankl, Victor.
  ### MAN'S SEARCH FOR MEANING.
  New York: Touchstone, 1984.

- Grossman, David.
  ### YELLOW WIND.
  London: Cape, 1988.

- Griffin, John Howard.
  ### BLACK LIKE ME.
  New York: Harper & Row,1979.

- Joubert, Elsa.
  ### THE LONG JOURNEY OF POPPIE NONGENA.
  Johannesberg: Jonathon Bell, 1989.

- Keenan, Brian.
  ### AN EVIL CRADLING.
  London: Vintage, 1993.

- Leddy, Mary Jo.
  ### PROMISES OF WAR, PROMISES OF PEACE.
  Toronto: Lester, Orphen, Denny's, 1990.

- Levi, Primo.
  ### IF THIS BE A MAN.
  London: Abacus, 1987.

- Lu, Li.
  ### MOVING THE MOUNTAIN.
  London: MacMillan, 1977.

- Narayan, Jayaprakash.
  PRISON DIARY.
  Seattle:University of Washington Press, 1977.

- McCarthy, John.
  SOME OTHER RAINBOW.
  London: Gorgi, 1993.

- Ratushinskaya, Irina.
  GREY IS THE COLOUR OF HOPE.
  London: Sceptre,1989.

- Rittner, Carol.
  BEYOND THE DIARY:
  Anne Frank in the World.
  Derry: YES! Publications, 1993.

- Rittner, Carol and Sondra Myers, eds.
  THE COURAGE TO CARE.
  New York: New York University Press, 1986.

- Tawil, Raymonda Hawa.
  MY HOME, MY PRISON.
  London: Zed Press, 1983.

- Timmerman, Jacobo.
  PRISONER WITHOUT A NAME
  CELL WITHOUT A NUMBER.
  New York: Penguin, 1986.

- Tutu, Desmond, et al.
  HOPE & SUFFERING.
  London: Fount, 1984.

- Waite, Terry.
  TAKEN ON TRUST.
  Cornet Books: London, 1994.

- Wielavatna, Usha.
  BEYOND THE KILLING FIELDS:
  Voices of Nine Cambodians in America.
  Stanford: University Press, 1993.

- Wiesel, Elie.
  NIGHT.
  New York: Hill & Wang, 1962.

- Wilson, Gordon, with Alf McCreary.
  MARIE, A STORY FROM ENNISKILLEN.
  London: Marshall Pickering, 1990.

Index